your special wedding toasts

sharon naylor

SOURCEBOOKS CASABLANCA™
AN IMPRINT OF SOURCEBOOKS, INC.®
NAPERVILLE, ILLINOIS

Published by Sourcebooks, Inc.

P.O. Box 4410, Naperville, Illinois 60567-4410

(630) 961-3900

FAX: (630) 961-2168

www.sourcebooks.com

Naylor, Sharon.
  Your special wedding toasts / by Sharon Naylor.
     p. cm.
  Includes bibliographical references.
  ISBN 1-4022-0268-7 (alk. paper)
  1. Wedding toasts. 2. Wedding etiquette. I. Title.
  PN6348.W4N39 2004
  808.5'1—dc22

                          2004000595

Printed and bound in the United States of America

QW   10 9 8 7 6 5 4 3 2 1

CONTENTS

For my mom,
Who always has the right words to say.

Acknowledgments

As always, a big thank you to my agent Meredith Bernstein and to my editor Deborah Werksman at Sourcebooks for bringing this book and this series to life.

Special thanks to all those who contributed their own real-life toasts to this collection, and to all those who shared stories about the toasts they received from others.

For everyone who was even a small part of this project: May all of your greatest dreams come true as well.

Introduction

A wedding toast is a big moment.

It could be the very first toast of the reception, setting the stage for the entire party to follow and striking a big emotional chord with everyone in the room.

It could be priceless words between the bride and groom, between parents and their son or daughter, between friends, or between children and their new stepparents. No one forgets a particularly touching toast made to their happiness, their health, and their future, and no one forgets how gratifying it is to have a friend or a relative be the one speaking those words. So the wedding toast you're preparing right now to make at a wedding…it's a big moment waiting to happen.

You might be a bit nervous right now, thinking, *How will I find the right words to say? How can I make my toast touching, but not sappy? Can I make everyone laugh?* or *How do I keep from stumbling all over my words?*

Relax! This book will help you through the entire process, starting with a brainstorming questionnaire that will help you collect and organize your thoughts and the stories you'll share, and then you'll go on to consider popular and inspiring quotes, plus the examples of real-life toasts that have been submitted by best men, grooms, brides, maids of honor, parents, and friends. I've also written a collection of completely original wedding toasts that can be delivered by the various major players in the wedding party, including some tailored to second weddings, outdoor and destination weddings, and even post-elopement parties.

DON'T PAY FOR IT!

There are many websites where you can *pay* to have someone create your toasts for you, and I know one couple who spent $600 to have a *professional writer* pen their toasts to one another.

While I'm not going to knock the fine work of professional speech writers, nor the time-and-effort-saving marvels of technology, I highly recommend that you write your own toasts so that they're perfect for you and for the bride and groom. It means so much more to the couple when the words come from *your* heart and it will mean so much more to *you* when you compose and deliver the ideal speech.

Part of what's going to make your toast great is your personality and your way with words. So take the writings in this book, mix your choices up with your personal style and character-filled personal anecdotes about the guest(s) of honor, and get ready to make a great impression when you lift your toasting flute to the happy couple. You're going to be great!

Ready to get started? Let's get going...

Part One:

The Basics of a Great Toast

Where It All Began

Even the experts can't quite pinpoint when and where in time and culture the practice of raising one's glass with words of well-wishing began.

Earliest man may have used ceremonial drinks as offerings to the gods of weather and hunting. The ancient Greeks and Romans would lift their goblets and speak to the gods, hoping to gain favor. The Romans' practice of moistening stale bread in their wine may have left the wine glass with the title "toast." There is also a legend of two revelers accidentally spilling some of their libation into each other's glasses, then drinking to good health. And finally the 17th century British were the leaders in toasting to the women beginning with the Queen.

There you have it...the various, diverse explanations on the origin of the toast. It's only natural that so much of early wedding lore was built around superstitions and gaining the favor and protection of the gods or good spirits. Those who wished the couple good fortune only naturally lifted their glasses and sealed their wishes with a sip.

Who Gives a Toast?

It used to be that the best man held the honor of giving the first and perhaps only official toast at the wedding celebration, but times have definitely changed. While the best man is still the premiere toast-maker at the party, he is very likely to be followed by the maid of honor, the father of the bride, the bride herself, and any number of other attendees.

In addition, the wedding reception is not the *only* place where toasts are proposed. From the moment that engagement ring finds a permanent home on the bride-to-be's finger, let the champagne corks pop, the wine bottles open and breathe, and the words of congratulations and best wishes start flowing. Here are some great opportunities for you and others to propose toasts:

When bride and groom first get engaged. Hopefully the groom has arranged for a bottle of bubbly or a fine wine that he and his now-intended can enjoy together to savor the biggest moment in their lives thus far.

When the parents find out. Hopefully, the engagement is good news for the parents, who might grab that bottle of White Star they've been saving for a special occasion.

When friends find out. In this global society, brides and grooms might live far from their parents and family, so the "family of location" could be the ones to order up that champagne.

The engagement party. This is where the major toasts are made by the parents who will welcome the fiancé or fiancée and their relatives into their own family and wish the couple well.

Bridesmaids luncheons. The maids will often trek down to the bridesmaids boutique for the trying-on of dresses, shopping for accessories and shoes, or just generally getting together to blow off some wedding steam. When the ladies do lunch, it could be time for a girlfriends toast…or two…or three.

Bridal showers. Whether they're parties of the all-female or co-ed variety, bridal showers are the ideal place for proposing toasts.

Wedding weekend activities. Weddings are all about the gathering of friends and family who love the couple, so more and more couples are extending the time they get to spend with these precious people in their lives. Rather than just have all of their guests show up for the wedding day—and maybe only get a few minutes during the course of the reception to speak with them—couples are planning several additional events throughout the weekend of their wedding. At any lunches, brunches, dinners, softball or mini-golf tournaments, cultural outings, or hikes through the state forest, glasses can be lifted for toasts.

The rehearsal dinner. With all the major wedding day players gathered together to run through the elements of the ceremony, the post-practice dinner is the perfect place for the bride and groom to propose a toast of thanks to everyone who helped them plan along the way, to their guests who traveled long distances to be present with them, to their parents for their help and guidance throughout their lives, and to one another at the start of the eighteen-hour countdown. Parents and grandparents might step up to say a word, as will the bridal party. In this more relaxed atmosphere, with the bride and groom's closest in attendance, this is where the best of toasts are often performed...and where the tears may flow more readily than in grand mixed company.

The morning prep-centers. If the bride and her ladies will go to a salon for their hair, makeup and nails to be done, they might enjoy a glass of champagne during their primping hours. Or, they'll drink to a few toasts at a bridal breakfast before it's time to step into their gowns and smile for the cameras. The men, as well, might stop off for a quick drink after their round of golf or during their dressing and primping time. These last-minute toasts make the most of last-minute excitement and can quell last-minute jitters as well. Just be sure to propose your toast to the bride *before* she gets her makeup done. You don't want tears streaming down her face from your perfect, touching speech five minutes before she walks down the aisle.

Before the reception. After the "I Do's" are uttered, the first kiss as husband and wife exchanged, the wedding rings slipped on, and all that birdseed thrown by the guests, bride and groom might find themselves alone for a valuable few minutes. They might be in the limousine with a bottle of champagne at the ready, and this is the perfect time to propose private toasts to one another, for their ears only. Or, if they'll head home for pictures to be taken, a quick toast for just the couple, the parents, and the bridal party to share would be a great moment with the Inner Circle. If the wedding couple and the bridal party will *not* join their guests for the cocktail hour, but will instead enjoy their own private one in a separate room, then break out the toasting flutes and allow everyone—or a spokesperson for the group—to say a few words before the all-inclusive celebration begins.

Before the cake cutting. Sure, the reception opened with the best man's speech, perhaps the maid of honor's, and the parents'—everyone but the limo driver has had his or her say, it seems!—but the moment right before the cake cutting is the *perfect* time for the bride and groom to take the microphone and propose a toast to all of their guests for coming, their parents for helping to plan the wedding (and perhaps paying for it!), and their friends for being so important to them. When the cake is wheeled out, everyone in the room is focused on this traditionally big moment at the reception, so it's the ideal time to speak.

Before bride and groom depart. If they haven't already, now would be a good time to toast family and friends, and to wish everyone a safe ride home.

At the after-party. The hot trend now is *not* to end the party when the reception closes down. Now, the bride, groom, and their closest guests continue on to a lounge, a hotel suite, even a karaoke bar for a post-reception party. Toasts made at this separate event have the advantage of coming after about...oh, let's say...five hours of drinking at the reception. You're going to hear a lot of "I love you, man!"... "No, I love *you*!" Be sure to bring the video camera along for these unforgettable toasts.

The morning after. If the parents or the couple will host a morning-after breakfast or brunch, then another toast could be in order—to the couple's happiness, to safe travels home, to gratitude for such a close group of friends and family, to the hosts. Whatever the topic, lift that mimosa and put a classy, elegant end to a classy, elegant wedding weekend.

On the honeymoon. For bride and groom only, special toasts during their most elegant dinners out, or lunches by the azure blue sea, will be remembered forever.

WHO GETS TO SPEAK?

Finally, we get to the speaker's list. The following guests of honor are welcome—at the bride and groom's discretion and permission, of course—to propose a toast at the wedding, and/or at any pre- or post-wedding activities:

* *the best man*
* *the maid (or matron) of honor*
* *the bride's father*
* *the groom's father*
* *the bride's mother*
* *the groom's mother*
* *the bride's sibling(s)*
* *the groom's sibling(s)*
* *the bridesmaids as a group, with one spokesperson or all saying a few words*
* *the groomsmen or ushers, with one spokesperson or all saying a few words*
* *the bride and groom*
* *the bride by herself*
* *the groom by himself*
* *grandparents of bride and/or groom*
* *godparents of bride and/or groom*
* *guardians of bride and/or groom*
* *the person or people who originally introduced the bride and groom to one another*
* *close relatives, like a favorite great-uncle*
* *cousins*
* *best friend*
* *groups of friends, like the bride's sorority sisters or the groom's childhood buddies*
* *college roommates*
* *bosses*
* *coworker friends*

* the couple's child or children
* the wedding officiant

The most important thing for anyone on the list of wedding-day toasters is *willingness*. The bride and groom might ask special relatives or friends to say a few words, and if this is the case, then the person they're asking has to be completely willing and able to write and deliver a great toast.

Very often, however, this isn't something the bride and groom map out before the wedding day. Some couples leave it to spontaneity—whoever would like to make a toast can do so. It's all going to be a wonderful surprise, as the best parts of weddings are very often the unplanned moments and gestures.

The Toasters Become the Toastees

Hang on to this list, since these are not only people who can give a toast, but they're also people who may be toasted by anyone on the guest list. Major points can be earned if the bride toasts her new mother-in-law publicly, or the groom his new father-in-law, the bride her new husband's friends, or the bride's parents toasting the groom's parents in a wonderful family bond.

Although...

Your greatest fear and frequent nightmare might be that your drunk, rambling, attention-craving uncle/sister/father/friend might embarrass herself and you by clinking her glass and causing a very cringe-worthy moment. Or, you might fear that a recently married couple on your guest list who eloped a few months ago, and didn't have a reception of their own, might use your reception as their moment in the spotlight. Or, that the groom's disgruntled ex might show up to publicly share some shocking revelation about him or you.

Whatever your wedding toast fear, rational or irrational, the solution is simple: just tell your band leader/deejay/emcee that *all* toast requests have to be okayed by either you or by a responsible family member. It sounds a bit controlling, but you'd be surprised how much nervous brides and grooms appreciate the relief of knowing there's some sort of filter in place. It might not stop a guest from rising to his or her feet, clinking a glass and speaking anyway, but at least you'll stop the ones who head for the microphone.

If the worst does happen and a guest makes a complete ass out of himself or herself, just take it in stride. The most gracious wedding couples just smile and shake their heads even when a guest does the unthinkable and speaks badly about them. Give it a second and the bridal party will swoop them right out of the room. The key is not to let it shake you. That person has just been an embarrassment to himself or herself, not to you. Act like it doesn't bother you and everything gets right back on track.

3

Who Are You Toasting?

When you raise your glass to anyone—whether it's the bride and groom, the parents, the chef—the one key ingredient for success is making it personalized. Your toast has to pay homage to *their* personalities, character, their history with you, and what makes them so incredibly special to you. Sure, you could just read a poem wishing them happiness (i.e., "May you always have love in your life, and may you always have life in your love."), but if that's all you say then your toast falls flat. You'll hear crickets. If not yawns. You've fallen on your face.

Don't take the cookie-cutter route and prove to everyone just how little imagination you have and how little effort you're willing to expend. Make your toast completely personalized and watch everyone's eyes light up.

Let's take the bride and groom as examples, since they'll be most often toasted. You'll talk about how you met the one with whom you're closest, like the groom, for instance. You'll talk about how you and he met in grade school, on the playground. You were both always picked last for dodgeball (audience laughs). But you both grew that summer, and you

Ouch! Too Personal!

On the flip side, there is such a thing as getting *too* personal. For instance, your time at the microphone is not the time to say:

"Jenny and I have been friends since college. I've seen her through really tough times, like the time she was so depressed she couldn't get out of bed for months. But she met Todd and now she's happy."

Jaws will drop and Jenny's going right back to her bed after a humiliation like that. So steer clear of the controversial, the dirty road to a laugh, and anything beyond a good-natured ribbing.

became the stars of your Little League team. You always looked up to your friend the groom because he was a team player even then. He taught you how to play fair, how to cooperate, how to get to second base...which came in handy in high school (audience laughs at innuendo). He was like your big brother all these years. You chased frogs together when you were young, you chased girls when you were older (bride nudges groom playfully), and you still compete even now. But now, he's finally one-upped you and found the girl of his dreams (assuming you're not married or engaged or "taken"). You couldn't imagine a woman better for him than (*bride's name*), you're proud to share him with her, and he's a better person because he's met her, etc.

The good toast has to be about the one you're toasting. Lose sight of that and you could make a tragic mistake:

1. Your toast is all about *you*. It's a common mistake made by people who are nervous about toasting. It becomes, "*I* spent my childhood growing up with the groom, and *I* learned so much from him. *My* life is better for knowing him, and *I* wish him all the best." That's very nice, but you've completely left him out of the picture! Get rid of the *I* and talk about him in relation to you. When you write your speech, count the number of times you say *I* just to get a feel for the balance of focus.

2. You forget about the bride. I attended a wedding recently where the best man gave a great, heartfelt speech about his friendship with the groom, how they saw each other through some tough family tragedies, how much they learned from one another and enjoyed belonging to one another's families like brothers. It really was quite moving and brought tears to the guests' eyes. Even the best man and groom teared up. As much of a home run as his speech was to the groom, the bride wasn't even a part of it. She got tacked on at the end of a three-minute speech with a second-thought expression of "All the best to you and Wendy, buddy." Remember: if you're toasting the couple, be sure to toast the *couple*.

So what is it about the couple that should be brought into this spotlight moment? No matter who you are or what role you play in the wedding, any speeches about the bride and groom generally cover what they were like as they were growing up, how much you admire them, the fun moments you've shared together, what you know of their childhood dreams, how proud you are to know them, what you wish for them.

Your mind might be a jumble right now since there's just so much you could say about them. Let me help you organize your thoughts with the following questionnaire. Take your time while filling this out. Come back to it a few times if you need to. But use it just to get out everything you *might* say, so that you can narrow it down to what you *will* say. The questions will guide you in the right direction...

Toast Questionnaire

1. When and how did you meet the person you are toasting? How long have you known one another?
2. Describe how your friendship/relationship grew over the years...
3. What does this person mean to you?
4. What are some of your favorite memories with this person?
5. What were your first impressions of the bride/groom when this person first introduced you?
6. Was there something this person said that made you think, "Ah, now this one is different!"
7. How did you know it was love between them?

Was there an instance? Something your friend said or did? Or didn't say or do anymore?

8. What makes the bride and groom so perfect for each other?

9. What do you admire most about their relationship?

10. Which better qualities does this relationship bring out in your friend? How has he/she grown and evolved as a result of being so in love?

11. How does their relationship inspire you and everyone else?

12. What do you wish for the happy couple?

Once you've worked through this questionnaire, you've undoubtedly brought out many memories, stories, and sentiments that would make a perfect part of your toast. And you'll find that once you start, it gets easier and easier to roll out the anecdotes. The more you come up with about this person, this couple, the better. It gives you plenty of raw material to start with, lots of rich material that just speaks of the people they are, and the makings of a great, personalized wedding toast.

What If You Don't Know the Bride Very Well?

How can you speak about someone you barely know? Sure, you might have been friends with the groom for twenty-plus years, but he went off to

Australia for work and came home a year later with a fiancée you aren't going to meet until the weekend of the wedding. All you know about her is that she has red hair, she's cute, smart, works as an investment banker, and can surf better than the groom can. How do you make a toast out of that?

It's a dilemma that's striking more often these days, as our global society is transporting us all over the world for work or play, far from our families and friends. We maintain our relationships through phone calls and email since we don't all live in the same town anymore. In fact, at many weddings today guests show up having never met the bride or the groom before. (That's an important factor for more than one reason—and I'll get back to it in a minute.)

If you don't know the other half of the happy couple very well, there are several ways to handle that. One is to just *be honest* about it. Say, "Mike called from Australia a few months after he landed there, and he said he was in love. He said she was beautiful, smart, funny, way better at surfing than he was, and he knew at first sight that this was the woman he was going to marry. I haven't had much time to get to know Sheila before today, but I know my friend, and I can tell by the way he describes her that she's absolutely perfect for him. And I'm sure we'll all spend the rest of our lives getting to know and love Sheila like Mike does."

It's simple, it's to the point, and it pays incredible homage to the lovely Sheila. And it's honest.

Another direction might be for you to talk to people who do know the bride. If you're the one out in Australia, best friends with the groom, while everyone back home has been enjoying Sheila's company for years, your best bet is to talk to the groom, his mother, his sisters, his father, your other friends. Find out more about this Sheila, and find out how Mike's been on his best behavior since he first met her. And then be honest about your research: "I can tell from our conversations that Mike's in love, real love. And everyone back home tells me that it's all because of Sheila. She brings out the best in him with her sense of humor and the way she doesn't take things too seriously. And I hear she can surf way better than he does."

Again, simple, honest, and with integrity. You don't pretend to know Sheila well yourself, but you reflect her qualities and the great effect she has on your friend.

No matter the research method, your tribute to the unknown bride (or groom) should always end with welcoming her to the family, to your group of friends, and to the world that the groom walks in when he's home. Let her know that you take a real interest in getting to know her better as you wish the two of them all the best. Now that's a great moment for the bride to experience.

It's All About Them

When toasting the wedding couple, *you* have the distinction of setting the tone for the entire wedding celebration. The couple has gone to great lengths to plan a wedding that's truly *them*...from the location to the menu to the entertainment to ethnic and cultural tributes to the monogram design on their cake. And you're the opening act. It's *you* who points the start of the reception towards *them*. And your toast is what does it.

Remember, as I said earlier, we live in a global society. Some wedding guests have come very far to attend the wedding, and they might have never met the bride or groom before this night. The first thing they'll hear about the bride or the groom is what *you* say. That's right, the bride's first impression to half of the groom's family might be what you say about her. It does happen. And it's one thing that many bridal party members forget—that suggestive story about how much the groom dated around in college...well, that's the first impression he makes on the bride's very protective male cousins, uncles, and her grandmother from Italy.

I don't bring this up to make you more nervous. I just want to remind you that there's a lot riding on your opening toast. You set the tone, you make a lasting first impression on behalf of the bride and groom. It's up to you to keep these things in mind as you sort through all the potential things you could say in tribute and blessing to the happy couple.

So What's *Them*?

Now that you've been warned off the questionable

anecdotes, the next topic when creating a toast that's all about the bride and groom is the *tone*. What *kind* of toast is their style?

If the couple are fun-loving with a great sense of humor between them, they're going to appreciate a toast that's more on the humorous side, or at least has humorous touches, more than they might a more serious, sentimental speech. The more serious couple, in the same way, might not be able to relate to a tongue-in-cheek semi-roast designed to get the crowd laughing at and with them. So know your subjects well before you plan out your speech, and make it something that fits *them* perfectly.

When You're Toasting Others

Toasts to parents, grandparents, the new in-laws, or good friends also need to be tailored to the recipients. So when you're writing a touching tribute to Grandma, think about her personality. She might be an Old-Worlder and value a more respectful tip of the hat to the family matriarch. Or, she might have a zipping sense of humor and appreciate a good joke at her expense. Toasting your friends? Make it as funny as they are. Throw in specially chosen anecdotes that share your best times together, and then bring on the tears when you thank them for their many years of laughter, comfort, celebration, support, and inspiration. You know your toastees—tailor your toasts to their natures.

4

Where to Find Inspiration

If you've ever given a speech or made a presentation at work, school, or a club, you might already know the wisdom of opening with a quote...or a joke. Something to catch the listener's attention and something with a theme to build your speech around. The same theory works with wedding toasts. As you'll read more about in chapter 5, you only have a few seconds at the start of your speech to grab your listeners and pull them in, get them interested in what you're saying and eager to hear more. A good start can often lead to a great finish.

In this chapter, you'll find a collection of quotes and sayings that you can use to springboard your own toast. Open with them, close with them, use them in the middle of your speech to emphasize your point. Take them and twist them to suit the honored guest. Follow them up with a well-planned punchline to get a laugh. The options are endless, so explore the following sayings—and others you might find!

QUOTES AND SAYINGS
To the Bride and Groom
"Now you will feel no rain, for each of you will be shelter for

the other. Now you will feel no cold, for each of you will be warmth to the other. Now there will be no loneliness, for each of you will be companion to the other. Now you are two persons, but there is only one life before you. May beauty surround you both in the journey ahead and through all the years. May happiness be your companion and your days together be good and long upon the earth."

—Apache wedding saying

"If a man really loves a woman, of course he wouldn't marry her for the world if he were not quite sure that he was the best person she could by any possibility marry."

—Geoffrey Chaucer

"Love is the flower you've got to let grow."

—John Lennon

"Think not because you are now wed that all your courtship is at an end."

—Antonio Hurtado de Mendoza

"If I choose to bless another person, I will always end up feeling more blessed."

—Marianne Williamson

"Man gets nothing brighter than a kind wife."

—Semonides

"Marriage is three parts love and seven parts forgiveness."

—Langdon Mitchell

"A successful marriage is an edifice that must be rebuilt every day."

—Andre Maurois

"Married couples who love each other tell each other a thousand things without talking."

—Chinese proverb

"If there is such as thing as a good marriage, it's because it resembles friendship rather than love."

—Michel de Montaigne

"We attract hearts by the qualities we display. We retain them by the qualities we possess."

—Jean Suard

"To love someone deeply gives you strength. Being loved by someone deeply gives you courage."

—Lao Tzu

"If you would be loved, love and be lovable."

—Benjamin Franklin

"Life isn't a matter of milestones, but of moments."

—Rose Kennedy

"The goal of marriage is to give the best years of your life to the spouse who *makes* them the best years of your life."

—Anonymous

"From every human being there arises a light that reaches straight to heaven. And when two souls that are destined to be together find each other, their streams of light flow together, and a single brighter light goes forth from their united being."

—Baal Shem Tov

"Love recognizes no barriers. It jumps hurdles, leaps fences, and penetrates walls to arrive at its destination full of hope."

—Maya Angelou

"Blessed are the man and woman who have grown beyond themselves."

—Psalm I

"Above all, let your love for each other be constant, for love covers a multitude of sins."

—I Peter 4:8

The Bride and Groom's Toasts to One Another

"Miracles occur naturally as expressions of love."

—Marianne Williamson

"My true love hath my heart and I have his."

—Sir Philip Sidney

"We are shaped and fashioned by what we love."

—Johann Wolfgang von Goethe

"It is the true season of love when we know that we alone can love; that no one could ever have loved before us and that no one will ever love in the same way after us."

—Johann Wolfgang van Goethe

"My bounty is as boundless as the sea.
My love as deep. The more I give to thee,
The more I have, for both are infinite."

—William Shakespeare

"Immature love says: 'I love you because I need you.'
Mature love says: 'I need you because I love you.'"

—Erich Fromm

"Life is worth the living of it. Do it with your whole heart."

—Maya Angelou

"This is my beloved, and this is my friend."
—Song of Solomon 5:16

"How do I love thee? Let me count the ways!
I love thee to the depths and breadth and height
My soul can reach, when feeling out of sight
For the ends of Being and ideal Grace.
I love thee to the level of every day's
Most quiet need, by sun and candlelight.
I love thee freely, as men strive for Right;
I love thee purely, as they turn from Praise.
I love thee with the passion put to use
In my old griefs, and with my childhood's faith.
I love thee with a love I seemed to lose
With my lost saints. I love thee with the breath,
Smiles, tears, of all my life! And if God choose,
I shall but love thee better after death."
—Elizabeth Barrett Browning

"Grow old along with me,
the best is yet to be."
—Robert Browning

"What the world really needs is more love and less paper-work."
—Pearl Bailey

"When you realize you want to spend the rest of your life with someone, you want forever to start as soon as possible."
—from *When Harry Met Sally*

"Oh, the comfort, the inexpressible comfort
of feeling safe with a person,
having neither to weigh thoughts nor measure words,
but pouring them all right out, just as they are,

chaff and grain together;
certain that a faithful hand will take and sift them,
keep what is worth keeping,
and then with the breath of kindness blow the rest away."
—Dinah Maria Mulock Craik

To Parents

"There is no more lovely, friendly, and charming relationship, communion or company than a good marriage."
—Martin Luther

(You can follow this up with words on how the parents' marriage inspired you.)

"The heart that loves is always young."
—Greek proverb

To Friends

"One of the most beautiful qualities of true friendship is to understand and be understood."
—Seneca

"A friend is one that knows you as you are,
understands where you have been,
accepts what you have become,
and still, gently allows you to grow."
—William Shakespeare

"Friends...
They cherish one another's hopes.
They are kind to one another's dreams."
—Henry David Thoreau

"My best friend is one who brings out the best in me."
—Henry Ford

"What is a friend? One soul in two bodies."

—Aristotle

"Love...has the greatest power, and is the source of all our happiness and harmony, and makes us friends with the gods who are above us, and with one another."

—Plato

"If you haven't learned the meaning of friendship, you haven't really learned anything."

—Muhammad Ali

International Toasts

Throw in a little bit of the wedding's ethnic or cultural flavor by ending your toast with one of these international calls to drink:

Brazil: *Saude!*—Cheers!

British: Cheers!

Chinese: *Chu nin chien kang!*—Wishing you good health!

Danish: *Skal!*—Cheers!

Dutch: *Prost!*—To your health!

Finnish: *Kippis!*—Cheers!

French: *A votre sante!*—To your health!

German: *Prost!* or *Prosit!*—To your health!

Greek: *Yasas!*—Cheers!

Hebrew: *L'Chaim!*—To life!

Irish: *Slainte!*—Cheers!

Italian: *Alla Salute!*—To your health!

Japanese: *Kan pai!*—Empty your glass!

Polish: *Sto lat!*—Live to a hundred!

Portuguese: *A sua saude!*—To your health!

Russian: *Na zdorovie!*—Be healthy!

Spanish: *Salud!*—To your health!

Swahili: *Furah!*—Be happy!

Swedish: *Skal!*—Cheers

5

The Twenty Keys to a Great Toast

It's all about the delivery. It's your big moment and all eyes are on you. Makes your heart pound, doesn't it? Well, don't worry...even if public speaking is one of your greatest fears, you can put your nerves to rest and deliver a terrific, unforgettable speech.

In this section, I've collected the top twenty tips for giving not only a good toast, but a *great* toast. It just takes a few preps and a little bit of a pep talk to get yourself ready. Here goes...

1. *Know thyself.* You can't stand up and deliver any speech that isn't of your own personal style. If you're a naturally witty person, then don't try to hide that to deliver a serious, sentimental toast. Be yourself, relax, and deliver your style of toast your way.

2. *Write it down.* I just shudder when I hear a best man, a maid of honor, a father of the bride or the bride and groom say they just plan to "wing it." While spontaneity is a wonderful thing, there's no place for that with wedding toasts. Do yourself a favor

and face high-tension nerves with the help of a written and early-prepared toast.

3. *Don't read word for word.* Reading word for word comes off as stilted, not at all natural, and provides absolutely no connection between yourself, the honored guests, and the crowd. Instead, print out cards with key words, phrases, and topics on it, and allow yourself to talk naturally using them as a guide.

4. *Keep it short and sweet.* Nobody likes it when someone goes on for too long. So be brief and to the point. You can capture a lot of emotion in fewer words.

5. *Introduce yourself.* Just your name and how you know the bride and/or groom is enough to make your greeting in the room. The guests want to know who you are.

6. *Open strongly.* You've got everyone's full attention, but if you don't give them something intriguing and engaging in the first fifteen to twenty seconds, you're a goner. So open with a quote, a funny anecdote, or a well-chosen joke.

7. *Have some structure to your speech.* A well-produced toast has a beginning, a middle, and an end. So break your script down into an opener, shared thoughts on the couple, and a closer of wishing them well.

8. *Make sure it flows.* A great speech has its thoughts connected with great transitions so that they move naturally from one to the next. As an example, you might start off talking about the

lovely Sheila and her surfing capabilities, and then go on with, "and speaking of handling any challenge with great balance and strength, Mike and Sheila have handled some very big challenges along the way…"

9. *Go for emotion…and not just one.* Your speech can lead the crowd from laughter to teary-eyed sentiment and back to laughter again. Make your toast an *experience* and you'll engage all listeners the entire length of your talk.

10. *Allow the tears to come.* Even the toughest best man has been known to get a bit choked up and need a second to compose himself. And that's a great thing! The power and love of friendship and family, plus the deep meaning of new marriage, *should* make you cry. So don't panic if the tears start welling. Trust me, everyone in the crowd will think you're terrific.

11. *Finish strong.* Tie back into your opening statement if you can to finish your speech off as if in a perfect circle. Complete the metaphors and bring the guests back to your opening quote.

12. *Don't forget to wish the couple well.* Again, don't forget the bride…your toast's intention is not only to honor your friend but to set the happy couple off on an adventure together.

13. *Look your best.* Present yourself flawlessly and your message won't be crowded out by people noticing that your top button is undone and you look very hot and uncomfortable.

14. *Slow it down*. Speak slowly and clearly. Being nervous tends to make speakers rush through, inviting stumbles and stutters, flipped wording, and the rise of panic. Just take your time.

15. *Breathe*. Again, being nervous can cause you to take more shallow breaths, and you might even get lightheaded from the lack of oxygen in your system. So stay calm by actively trying to breathe more deeply and slowly.

16. *Use the pause.* Great comics, actors, and public speakers have mastered the art of the "dramatic pause." Take a second to let your joke sink in, or lead up to a big point by taking just a few beats of silence beforehand. Play with the art of pause.

17. *Watch your stance.* Stand up straight and confident and don't shift your weight from foot to foot, as many people do unconsciously when they're nervous. Stand comfortably and own your space.

18. *Watch your hands.* Your hands give away your jitters level, so be mindful of not touching your hair too much, twisting your ring, taking your hands in and out of your pockets—all of these, again, are unconscious moves. Try to be aware of them.

19. *Make eye contact*. You want to connect with your audience and have them connect with you as well as what you're saying. The only way to do that is to make eye contact…with the bride and groom, of course, when you address them, and also with the audience. Scan the room, catch the eye of

several of your rapt listeners, smile, and continue owning the room.

20. *Smile!* Let your great personality show. The bride and groom chose you for this role and wanted you to speak to their guests because they knew you'd be great. So let your true self shine through. Even if you mess up, you'll still be adorable.

As an Added Bonus

So many toast-makers are taking their spotlight moment at the reception and presenting the bride and groom with a special surprise gift right there in front of all of their guests. At a recent wedding, the best man wheeled out a painting he knew the bride and groom had admired during their trip to the shore where they became engaged. On a tip from the groom, the best man had driven down to that gallery, bought the painting, and gave it to them right then as a gift from himself. There is no better closer to a best man speech than making a couple's wish come true and giving them something special right from the heart. Not a dry eye in the house on that one.

Remember, you don't have to be perfect. You're not being graded on your performance. And even bad wedding toasts can sometimes be so bad that they actually become quite adorable. The teasing you'll get from your friends will only last a few weeks...maybe months. It's not so bad. The entire crowd knows that you're human, that this is a pressure situation, and they're probably glad that it's you up there and not them! Everyone's pulling for the one making the toast and wants you to do well. If you're like most, you want to do well for the bride and groom's sake as well as for your own personal pride. And that can be pressure.

Relax. You're going to do fine. Just remember to practice over and over again so that you know your toast top to bottom. Make last-second changes if you wish to capitalize on something funny or touching that happened at the ceremony. The entire thing is completely in your control. And you're going to be great.

Part Two:

Lift Your Glass and
Your Pen!...Wedding
Toasts for Everyone

6

The Best Man's Toast

It's the first toast of the reception...the mood-setter. Our goal with this chapter is to make your best man speech absolutely ideal. You'll be able to say "they laughed, they cried...I owned the room."

And, it's ultimately even more wonderful to give the bride and groom a very precious gift...your thoughts and words coming from the heart. Especially for men, you don't often sit down with your guy friends and tell them how important they are to you. Expressing the sentimental stuff might be unfamiliar territory for you.

If you've already broken out into a sweat just reading about giving a toast, you're exactly like just about every other best man in history. The nerves do hit. Fear of public speaking, remember, is ranked highly on the big-time phobia list. But just relax! Go over the smart toasting tips in chapter 5 once again, and then concentrate on what you're going to say.

You can make them laugh...you can make them cry...you can own the room. Just be yourself and write a toast that says it all.

Been There, Done That

Some tuxedoed talkers don't consider themselves gifted writers, so they choose to stick with traditionally delivered toasts, those tried-and-true standards that have seen many a best man through in the past. There's nothing wrong with using an "oldie" that might have been used before as part of your toast. Even at the most untraditional wedding, a little dash of good old tradition might be enjoyable. So consider these conventional writings if you'd rather not pen an original:

"May your life always be filled with love, and may your love always be filled with life."

"A toast to love and laughter...and happily ever after."

"May your love last forever."

"Here's to the husband, and here's to the wife...May they always remain happy for life."

"Here's to the bride, and here's to the groom, and here's to every guest in the room."

"May the road rise to meet you, may the wind always be at your back, the sun shine warm upon your face, the rain fall soft upon your fields, and until we meet again may God hold you in the hollow of His hand."

—Traditional Irish saying

"May you live as long as you want and want nothing as long as you live."

"Here's to the health of the happy pair;
may good luck follow them everywhere;
and may each day of wedded bliss
be always as sweet and joyous as this."

"The path to happiness is this...Live well, laugh often, love much."

"May your hand be forever clasped in friendship, and your hearts forever clasped in love."

"Live for the future, learn from the past, and enjoy the present."

"My heart is as full as my glass, when I drink to you, old friend."

"Here's to your health.

May you make age curious,

Time furious

And the rest of us envious."

"May you be poor in misfortune, rich in blessings, slow to make enemies and quick to make friends."

"May your glasses be ever full. May the roof over your head be always strong.

And may you be in heaven half an hour before the devil knows you're dead."

"May the most you wish for be the least you get."

"May your troubles be less and your blessings be more. And nothing but happiness come through your door."

"May the blessings of light be upon you, light without and light within. And in all your comings and goings, May you ever have a kindly greeting from them you meet along the road."

CUSTOMIZING YOUR TOAST

Borrowing from others might not be for you. You might have enough confidence in your own ability to pen a toast that you don't need to sample anyone else's lyrics. Before you start digging in, let me give you a few Don'ts to help you avoid making a *big* mistake and embarrassing yourself as well as the couple:

* *Don't humiliate the groom or bride just to get a laugh.* There's a place for locker room stories and reminiscing about spring break, but this isn't it. And this is *not* the time to tease the groom about his bride being controlling, or to tease the bride about her not liking his Friday nights out with the boys. Be considerate and stay in good taste.

* *Don't leave out the crowd.* Make sure you preface any story you tell with at least some explanation that they can understand.

* *Don't talk cryptically.* The bride won't like it if you say something to the groom that's an obvious reference to some kind of past impropriety, and neither will anyone in the crowd.

* *Don't apologize for yourself before you speak!* This is the number one mistake that nervous best men make, starting them off awkwardly. The guests, and the guests of honor, are with you. They understand. So no apologies for not being the greatest public speaker.

* *Again, it's okay to get tears in your eyes.* And it's actually charming to see real emotions coming out of you. (A note to you from Best Man Ed in Chicago—"Bridesmaids love it when you're a sensitive guy.")

Now, let's get started...

"**May I have** everyone's attention? My name is Mike, and I am the best man. Jeff and I have been friends since the fourth grade...They called us 'Thunder' and 'Lightning' because we were trouble wherever we went. From BB gun fights to climbing trees and breaking our arms, to tormenting the girls on the playground and giving our teachers and our parents some pretty good-sized ulcers. And then we grew up...and now we have the ulcers. Graduate school, med school for Jeff, winning over our beautiful brides...

"It's been a great ride with you, Jeff. You've always been there for me, no matter what, and I'll always be there for you. You're like a brother to me, and you're like a son to my parents. I hope this is the start of many adventures for you and Tiffany. Cheers!"

"My name is Brian, and I am Ken's brother as well as the best man. Actually, Ken is the best man here today...He's won the heart of Patricia, he's taken the big step into marriage and he's proven to us all that he turned out pretty well. Those of us who have known him all his life are sitting here scratching our heads and saying, 'Now when did Ken get it together?' I have the answer to that one. It's when he found Patricia. If I can share a little story with you... Back when Ken first started dating Patricia, we all thought 'No chance, she's way too good for him.' She was cultured, while his idea of culture was going to Ozzfest. She was proper, while he still cut his spaghetti with a knife and fork. We thought she'd never take him. But then a strange thing started happening. Ken started *learning*. He said to me one day, 'I want to be good enough for her.' And he set off on a quasi-*Karate Kid* type makeover, getting the fashion thing down, learning his wines, learning to cook. He was still the same great guy inside...He just polished himself up for Patricia.

She brought out the best in him. And from what I'm told, he's expanded her horizons as well. Maybe opposites *do* attract.

"Whatever it is, we're all very happy that Ken and Patricia have blended themselves together and joined together for life. Knowing his giving heart and her gift for laughter, they'll be a very happy couple for a lifetime. I wish you all the best of everything, Ken and Patricia…Here's to you!"

"Good evening, everyone…Would you please stand and lift your glasses to Mark and Marianne, on this very big day that they've waited twelve years for. Marianne has the patience of a saint, and Mark has exquisite taste in women. It might have taken them a long time to get to the altar, but I know they've enjoyed every moment they've shared to this point, and that the wait was nothing to them. They're the best of friends, the life of the party, and the people you'll call if you need anything. Two great people found one another, and now they get to set off on a lifetime of happiness. Here's to you, Mark and Marianne…May your every minute of every day from now on be full of joy."

"Here's to Ryan and Celeste…a few words before we get this party started. First off, I am Chris, the best man, and I have been friends with Ryan since we met on the first day of college when we were moving in as roommates. I wasn't too sure about him when he started putting all kinds of professional wrestling posters up in the room, and I was even less sure of him when he started playing Duran Duran music—and singing along. But in time, over many midnight runs to the 7-Eleven for nachos and once I saw how easily he got along with the girls in the dorm, he got the OK stamp of approval. I've said it before, and I'll say it often...Ryan's the nicest guy anyone's ever met. He'd give you the shirt off his back, he'd give you the keys to his car, and he'd move you into your new place.

"It was my good fortune that the roommate lottery at the University of Delaware paired us up because I got a best friend for life. The only person in here who knows what I mean is Celeste. The University of Delaware hit one out of the park for her as well by putting the two of them in the same dorm together. Serendipity is what they call it when 'a fortunate accident' places you at the right place at the right time, so it was serendipity for all of us to meet like we did. Fate took over from there, and now Ryan and Celeste are husband and wife. So let's drink a toast to the happy couple, to serendipity and to fate, to all of us being here at the right place, at the right time, and to your happiness and to a long and happy, healthy life together."

Best Man Speaking for a Group Toast
"My name is Kent, and I'm speaking on behalf of all of the groomsmen when I say congratulations and all the best of wishes to Dennis and Veronica for a long and happy life together."

"May I ask you all to stand and raise your glasses to the happy couple? My name is Anthony, and I am the best man. The groomsmen—Mark, Donnie, Chip, and Ralphie—and I would like to wish Dan and Christine a very happy life together. Congratulations on your marriage, and know that we're all here for you whenever and wherever you need us.

"Here's to your happiness."

Let's Go to the Videotape!

A new trend in best man toasts *completely* removes the pressure of giving a live, stand-up speech. Instead of reading a toast in front of the guests, the best man creates a toast *presentation* on video or DVD. Expertly edited, these video productions feature a meaningful soundtrack and video footage of the groom and his buddy together during their football days, at college graduation, and for big lifetime moments of their time together. Either with a voice-over or standing in front of the camera, the best man delivers his funny, heart-touching toast. No pressure. No public speaking phobias. It's all a done deal before the wedding day even happens. All he does on the wedding day is push the Play button, sit back and watch the bride, groom, and their guests enjoy the show.

These video toasts are springing up all over the place, making the most of technology...and some best men even connect faraway friends and family who couldn't make it to the wedding to the ballroom and to the happy couple via Webcam, surprising the bride and groom with a live greeting from guests they didn't think could make it. It's a surprise that everyone loves.

7

The Maid of Honor's Toast

Somewhere in history, a brave maid of honor took tradition and threw it out the window by standing up after the best man gave his first-of-the-night toast to grab that microphone and give one of her own. It might have been shocking the first time that happened, and we'll never know who the first woman was to claim that spot for the ladies in the traditional toast lineup. But we're thankful to her because the maid or matron of honor has every right to make a best wishes toast of her own to the happy couple.

"May I have everyone's attention, please? My name is Sarah, and I am the maid of honor. Julie and I have been friends since the second grade, roommates in college, and we now live about a block apart. So Julie's been a big part of my life for my entire life. She very much *is* a sister to me and she's part of my family. We've shared adventures together, road trips, we bought our first bras together, lived through each other's big crushes and heartbreaks...and we've always been there for each other's shining moments...like today. It's been amazing to see Julie and Craig's relationship grow from their nervous first date, through the months where they were falling in love, to that night I'll never forget when Julie came home with that rock on her finger and the biggest smile I've ever seen on her. I adore Craig and couldn't want a better husband for her. So, Julie, thank you for being such a great friend and sister to me...and Craig, when you got Julie you got all of her friends to deal with...and thank you for always being so great and so generous with us. I know I speak for the rest of the girls when I say we all hope we find a guy just like you...and yes, we will be hitting on your brother tonight. Congratulations to the two of you. May your heart's every wish come true."

"If there are three things that I could wish for Anna and Brett, they would be a home filled with love, a life filled with family and friends, and an everlasting partnership that fulfills their every need. I've known Anna since forever, and I've never seen her so happy or so beautiful. Brett, you won the lottery when you won her heart. I wish you both all the best and a lifetime of joy."

"To Susan and Steve, and their forever filled with love, laughter, affection, and forgiveness. You both love each other so much, you've come so far together, you've overcome so much...This is the beginning of your Happily Ever After, and no one deserves it more than the two of you."

"I am Stephanie, the maid of honor, and like all of you, I'm so thrilled to be here today to see Kailey and Tom begin their marriage so beautifully. Kailey is, of course, my little sister. She was my little doll when she was born and I always looked out for her. Now tell me, have you ever seen a more gorgeous bride? Kailey, Tom...I love you both. You deserve all the blessings that life can give two people...and, like Mom, I can't wait for the time when you have kids—because two people who love each other and who love their friends and family as much as you do, two decent souls who'd do anything to help and support the people they love are going to be amazing parents. You have a great love between you...so here's to the great life you're sure to share."

Maid of Honor Speaking for the Group
"My name is Sarah, and I'm the maid of honor. On behalf of all the bridesmaids, Jenny, our junior bridesmaid, and Rose, the flower girl, I'd like to say congratulations to Marcy and Matt and hopes and wishes for a fabulous life together. Marcy, you've never looked more beautiful. And I'm just thrilled for you that your dream has come true. You've found your prince, and your happily ever after begins now. Matt, we love you and we love how you make Marcy happy. Here's to both of you...may you always be more and more in love each day."

"When Tina asked me to be her maid of honor, I literally jumped around for joy. Not just because I knew she had terrific fashion sense and would pick out some amazing dress for us girls to wear...not just because I knew I'd get to plan her bridal shower and stand up for her on her wedding day...but because I was finally going to get a chance to bring this out into the open. I have here in my hand a little something that Tina wrote when we were in the fifth grade, pathologically boy-crazy romantics who played Madonna songs and talked about our weddings right down to the kind of shoes we'd wear. We were really girly girls, and we loved it. Tina, even then being obscenely organized, decided to write down the qualities she wanted her future husband to have.

"Now keep in mind that this is Tina in the fifth grade talking here...

'I want him to be taller than I am...

I want him to be able to drive...

I want him to be nice to me...

He has to like swimming and tennis...

He will call me 'honey' and 'darling' and he will compliment what I do.

He has to be honest and not a cheater at anything...

He has to have dark hair and nice arms...

He has to have a nice voice to listen to...

He has to like holding my hand in public...

He can't dance like a spaz...

And he has to love me like my dad loves my mom.'

"I know we're all breathing a sigh of relief that Nick doesn't dance like a spaz and that he can drive and that he has dark hair...Tina, you put in your order, and you got the man of your dreams. If you made a list now, we're all sure that Nick would still fit the criteria, just as you'd fit his checklist. You're perfect together, a match made in Heaven, and I wish you all the good things you could ever want out of life. Here's to your happiness."

"For fifteen years, Jill and I have been the best of friends. A few years ago, Jill's job took her far away, so our daily chats over coffee turned to daily emails, and we didn't grow one inch apart. When Jill's emails started getting fewer and fewer a year ago—which means one every other day instead of every day—I didn't think she was fading as a friend or that the distance was making us grow apart, I knew she had fallen in love. Then one day, she wrote: 'I'm only saying this to you, because I'm afraid to say it out loud and jinx it, but I hope Pete is THE ONE.' And now he is. I'm unbelievably delighted to be standing here today as Jill's matron of honor, to finally meet this man I've read so much about, and to see Jill's wish turn into reality. Jill, you're a part of my heart at any distance, and seeing you so happy just thrills me. I wish you both a lifetime of love."

"My name is Emily, and I am Tara's sister. As many of you might know, Tara is a cancer survivor. She's the bravest and strongest woman I've ever known. She fought her way through her illness, keeping all of us optimistic instead of the other way around. And Brian was right there by her side. A lesser man might have become afraid and run from the gravity of her condition, but Brian was always there, even through the worst of it all. He held her hand as she slept, he brought her hats when she lost her hair, and he always told her she was beautiful. His devotion to her brought tears to our eyes, and his presence gave her more reason to fight. Now, Tara is cancer-free. And here is Brian holding her hand once again, on into forever. Tara has called him her angel, and no one here would disagree. For two people who love so strongly, who have such faith, who support each other so well, to begin a life together as husband and wife...That's Heaven-sent. Tara and Brian have already done their 'worst of times' and made it look effortless. So now here's to their 'best of times,' and a long, long lifetime of blessings for both of us. Tara, I love you...Brian, I love you too and welcome to the family."

8

The Bride and Groom's Toasts

If you're a bride or groom, this is the moment where you can express yourself more fully and freely than in the midst of your ceremony, where grandeur and tradition often rule and personalized vows can only go so far. Here, at your reception, perhaps after you've gotten a glass of champagne into you, you'll speak your heart to your new spouse in front of all of your loved ones and make an everlasting memory for you all.

Brides and grooms proposing toasts to one another is not a new thing. But it is a growing trend. In the past, brides and grooms often stood up together to thank their parents (more on that in chapter 9), and very often the groom has taken the microphone to address his lovely bride. Now, more and more, the brides are doing the same. So cruise through the samples in this section to help you create your own personalized toast to your own bride or groom...

A Toast for the Bride

"Monica, I am so happy and so proud to finally be able to call you my wife. You're just absolutely beautiful to me, inside and out, every day of the year. Thank you for saying yes, and for making me the happiest man alive."

"To my beautiful bride... You make me so happy—you have from the first moment I met you—and I will spend my lifetime doing everything I can to make you happy as well. I don't know what I did right to win a woman as amazing as you, so thank you for loving me all of these years."

"I am so blessed to call you my own. We've waited a long time for this day, and it's finally here. God smiled on me when He brought us together, and I know that we will spend our lives making Him proud of our partnership. You are my gift and my treasure...I will love you always."

"Karen, what can I say? You've made me the happiest man on earth today because I get to call you my wife. You came along during a tough time in my life and you stood by me. You taught me what unconditional love is all about and I have to thank you for that. You've brought so much to my life, and to my family...I love you so much, and I will always love you. So here's to our future, to our happiness, and to making all of our dreams come true."

"Mandy, you have given me so much. You've shared your life with me, you've shared your faith with me, you've shared your family, your goals, and your dreams with me. How could I ask for anything more? All I ask of you now is that you allow me to make you as happy as you've made me for the rest of our life together. I love you, sweetie. Thank you for saying yes, and for becoming my bride."

For the Groom

"Grant, you have made me the happiest woman on earth today. I've dreamed of this day since I was a little girl and I dreamed of the man I was going to marry. And although I never could have believed it, you are so much more than I ever imagined or dreamed for myself. You make me smile, you make me happy every day. And I can't wait for everything that's to come our way, for every adventure, every blessing to come—because I get to share them with you. You're the love of my life, and I'm so lucky to have found you."

"David, you make all of my dreams come true. You fill me with such joy and such comfort, you make me smile and laugh more than I ever have. And you've given me so much to remember and so much to look forward to. Our life together is going to be wonderful. I am your forever love, for always."

"Michael, when you asked me to marry you, I was on Cloud Nine. Even thought it may seem like I was all about planning the wedding, and even though I might have gotten a little bit crazy over it sometimes, the one thing I was always dreaming about and looking forward to was getting to spend my life with you. And now we have each other. Thank you for being mine, for always understanding me and always supporting me, being my soft place to land, and my favorite place to be. I love you."

"Kevin, you are my one true love. Today and always. This is the best day of my life, because I married my best friend."

Quotes to Borrow

Yes, you too can build your toast off of a well-known literary quote. In fact, the number 1 quote most often borrowed by brides and grooms for their toasts to one another is "Grow old along with me, the best is yet to be" by Robert Browning. No truer nor more appropriate words than these have ever been penned for a moment such as this. Read on to see if any others speak for you...

"If I know what love is, it is because of you."
—Hermann Hesse

"But here's the joy;
my friend and I are one...
then she loves but me alone!"
—William Shakespeare

"When you love someone, all your saved-up wishes start coming out."
—Elizabeth Bowen

"Your words dispel all of the care in the world and make me happy...they are as necessary to me now as sunlight and air...your words are my food, my breath, my wine—you are everything to me."
—Sarah Bernhardt

"Any time not spent on love is wasted."

—Torquato Tasso

"Coming together is a beginning.
Keeping together is progress.
Working together is a success."

—Henry Ford

"Everything comes to us from others. To be is to belong to someone."

— Jean-Paul Sartre

"Here's to Eternity...may we spend it in as good company as this night finds us."

—Author unknown

"You are all-beautiful, my beloved, and there is no blemish in you."

—Song of Solomon, 4:7

Even More Special

Now would be a great time to dedicate a song to one another, to dance a second dance to your second "our song," or to present your new spouse with a special gift or surprise. Seal this moment with something special that neither of you will ever forget.

9

Toasts to Parents

They birthed you, they raised you, they put you through school. They lived through your Terrible Twos and maybe even your Terrible Twenties. They nursed you when you were sick, cheered you when you were strong, comforted you when you were down, taught you, inspired you, drove you to soccer practice and Little League, Girl Scouts, and ballet class, vacationed at Disney World a dozen times instead of sailing the Mediterranean together, sat through your class plays, chaperoned field trips, taught you to drive...and helped to make you who you are today. Plus, they may have paid for your wedding. Mom and Dad certainly deserve a word of gratitude and love after all of that work, right?

They did it with love, but any parent who says "Oh, you don't have to thank me. That's what parents are for!" is just *dying* for a little bit of public recognition. The moment you acknowledge them and actually say the words we all say *way* too infrequently to our parents while they're alive is priceless. Your parents will *never*, ever forget...and neither will you. It's an immortal moment between parent and son or daughter, the golden threads of a lifetime.

To Mom and Dad

"For all you are, and for all you've done to make this day and every day sweeter...Thank you! We love you both very much."

"To the most wonderful parents on earth. I'm blessed to call you mine, blessed to have been guided and loved by you all of my life. Thank you for a lifetime of your love."

"Mom, Dad, thank you for everything you've done to help make this a wonderful day for us. And thank you for always being there for me, for showing me the first example I ever had of unconditional love, acceptance, support, generosity, and friendship. I couldn't have asked for a better family, just like I couldn't have asked for a better husband. All that I am, and all that I will become is due in part to the foundation you've given me. And I will always be grateful to you for that."

"Mom and Dad, I wanted to take a moment to thank you tonight, for all that you've given me throughout my life. You've taught me what love is all about...kindness and consideration, patience and forgiveness, always letting people know you love them both in word and in deed. Because of your example, and because of the loving home I was raised in with two parents who adored each other and their kids, I know that my marriage will be all the stronger. What you've given me is beyond measure, and there's no full way to express just how much I appreciate you. So this will have to do...I love you both very, very much."

"Mom and Dad, you always taught me to dream big, play hard, reach for the stars, and never let the first five No's stop you. It's with these and all other lessons you taught me that I've become who I am and that I won the hand and heart of my new bride. I have so much to thank you for... I love you. Here's to you."

"Mom, Dad, I probably wasn't the easiest of your kids to raise. In fact, I think you were probably understating it when you said I was a 'handful' growing up. Problem child was more like it. But you never gave up on me. Even at times when I didn't really know which way to turn, you were there, and it was always the right direction when I turned to you. Your unfailing devotion to me, support of me and love for me finally got me on the right track. So thank you for all of those sleepless nights, all of your tough love, your words of support, your unfailing efforts to help me find what *you* knew was inside of me. Job well done, Mom and Dad. Thank you for loving me so much when I was hard to love and for loving me so much now...I'll never forget what you did for me, and I'll always be here for you."

"Mom and Dad, first of all, *thank you* for everything you did to help plan the wedding of my dreams. I know that you've always been there, that you always did whatever it took to make my wishes come true, that you sacrificed so much and gave so much all along...And I've appreciated every single thing you've ever done for me. You're just terrific parents, and I am so very lucky to be standing here today with the best husband on earth, and with the best parents on earth. It doesn't get much better than this."

"**Mom, Dad,** you taught me the meaning of the word love, you taught me to believe in myself, to work hard to reach my goals, to hold true to my faith, to always remember that family is forever. The lessons you taught me make me who I am, and they make me a better person in this world. You both inspire me to greater things, greater character, greater strength, and greater hope. At this point in my life, these are the best wedding presents possible. All thanks to you. I love you both."

"**Mom and Dad...**Justin and I wanted to take a moment to thank you for everything you have done for us. We wouldn't be here without your love and generosity, your support, and your valuing of my dreams. So thank you for being all the greatest things that parents can be and for giving me a lifetime of happiness."

"**I have a lot to be** grateful for today...a wonderful new husband, a new exciting chapter of my life just beginning, that my family and friends are all here with us...and I have something else that I'm *incredibly* grateful for...the love of my parents, John and Cecilia Marshall. Mom, Dad, you have given me so much...so much love and support of everything I ever dreamed of doing. You gave me a warm and happy home to grow up in, so many fun memories of our family, a deep sense of my own value and worth. I know I am lucky to have spent my whole life with you in it, and I am luckier still to look forward to the rest of my life with you in it. I love you both...forever and always."

For Divorced and Remarried Parents

"Mom and Jeff, Dad and Kaila, I have been so fortunate to have *four* loving parents to guide me, love me, and support me all my life. This is the happiest day ever for me, more so because I get to share it with all of you. You all taught me the power of forgiveness and friendship, the bonds of love that grow like rose vines around those who care for a child, and the essence of what it means to seek happiness and share it with those around you. You have my love forever. Thank you for all you are to me, all you are to us, and—someday—all you will be to *our* children."

To the In-Laws

There's no better start to a marriage, family diplomacy-wise, than when the bride toasts to her groom's parents, and when the groom toasts to the bride's parents. Saluting the in-laws can pave a path to future harmony.

"I'd also like to thank Melissa's parents, Mr. and Mrs. Jorgenson, for raising such an incredible daughter and for making me feel so welcome in their family."

"I'd like to thank Matt's parents...first of all, for everything they did to help us with the wedding, and second of all for raising a true gentleman. They did a great job raising Matt to be a real man, to have family values and decency and chivalry…Those were the first things I loved about him, and while I got to know both of you in the beginning, I saw pretty quickly where he got those qualities. So thank you for raising the man of my dreams and for welcoming me into your home and your family."

To Mother

In case Mom hasn't become completely dehydrated by the amount of tears she's shed on the wedding day, you can almost guarantee additional tears of joy and gratitude with a toast devoted solely to her. Whether it's from her darling son or the daughter who's the light of her life, the words find a permanent place in a mother's endless vault of memories.

Quotes About Mothers

Here are a few quotes about moms that you might include in your toast to the woman who gave you life…

"All that I am, my mother made me."
—John Quincy Adams

"A mother is a mother still, the holiest thing alive."
—Samuel Taylor Coleridge

"God couldn't be everywhere, so he created mothers."
—Jewish proverb

"Men are what their mothers made them."
—Ralph Waldo Emerson

"Youth fades, love droops, the leaves of friendship fall. A mother's secret hope outlives them all."
—Oliver Wendell Holmes

"Yes, mother I can see you are flawed. You have not hidden it. That is your greatest gift to me."
—Alice Walker

"My mother (said) the tragedies of your life have the potential one day to be comic stories next."
—Nora Ephron

"My mother had a great deal of trouble with me, but I think she enjoyed it."
—Mark Twain

"A mother is the truest friend we have."
—Washington Irving

"A toast to my mother, who is so much more than a mom...she's also my friend. I love you."

"I am so blessed to have you for my mother. All of my life, you have been there for me, by my side to cheer me on, comfort me, guide me, give me the greatest words of advice...your love is unconditional, as is mine for you. You're a gift in my life, and I am so very thankful for you."

"To Mom...thank you for helping me all of these long months to plan this beautiful wedding. I know I drove you crazy calling all the time from school asking if you called the photographer, and if you called the florist. Thanks for putting up with me in all my stressed-out craziness and having the sense and the wisdom to know why I was freaking out like that. You said it would all come together, and it did. You said it would all be just as I'd dreamed, and it is. In case I haven't thanked you the million times you deserve, let me say it again...Thank you for your help with the wedding, for everything you've done for me, for everything you've done for us, and for just being you. I love you."

"Mom, you're the best! You work miracles every day. You single-handedly raised me and Theresa, and even in the tough times, you were always there for us. I thank God for giving me such a terrific, loving mother with a heart of gold. You did the work of two parents...no, make that about ten, and I thank you from the bottom of my heart for all you gave to me, all you hoped for me, and all you worked for me to have. Love you."

To Father

Quotes About Fathers

"When a father gives to his son, both laugh. When a son gives to his father, both cry."

—Jewish proverb

"I cannot think of any need in childhood as strong as the need for a father's protection."

—Sigmund Freud

"Noble fathers have noble children."

—Euripides

"The most important thing a father can do for his children is to love their mother."

—Henry Ward Beecher

"A man knows he is growing old, because he begins to look like his father."

—Gabriel Garcia Marquez

"By the time a man finally realizes his father might be right, he usually has a son who thinks he's wrong."

—Charles Wadsworth

"It's only when you grow up, and step back from him, or leave him for your own career and your own home—it's only then that you can measure his greatness and fully appreciate it."

—Margaret Truman

"One night a father overheard his young son saying his nightly prayers. 'Dear God,' said the little boy. 'Make me the kind of man my Daddy is.' Later that night, the man prayed, 'Dear God, please make me the man my son wants me to be.'"

—Author Unknown

"Dad, I wanted to say thank you...for everything you've been to me, for all the times we shared, for everything you taught me, and for being the best kind of father there is...one who's not afraid to show or tell his kids that he loves them."

"Dad, I love you. From way back when I was a little girl and you'd let me stand on top of your shoes while we danced, when we caught fireflies in the backyard, when you spent all those hours in the backyard teaching me to hit a softball. Did you know that my friends all said that I had the best father? That they wished they had dads like mine? I'm very lucky to have a father like you. I knew it when I was a little girl, and I know it now. Thank you."

"**My dad** taught me some of the most important lessons of my life. He taught me what it really means to be a man. Be true to your word. Always be on time. Open the door for a lady. Always admit when you're wrong. Pick yourself up and dust yourself off. Dad, your lessons got me where I am today, and they'll get me where I want to be in the future. And I'll always have you to thank."

Combination Toasts for Parents

It goes without saying that the timing of your toasts to parents can be spread out...stop the music at one point to honor the bride's parents and the groom's parents and then stop the music a half hour later to give a spotlight toast to your mother, and so on. Or you could combine them all and have "parent time" where you both thank the bride's parents, then the groom's parents, and each individual mom or dad you'd like to honor. The choice is yours. Spread out the love over the course of the day, or hit them with one big emotional wallop at once.

Want to bring down the house? Dedicate a special song to them right after your toast...say, their own wedding song for them to dance to or a song that reminds you of them. And pass the tissues!

10

Toasts by Parents, Grandparents, Godparents, and Others

Of course, your parents, grandparents, godparents, and any other people who are like parents to you might wish to grab the microphone to deliver their best...and perhaps share some amusing stories about your childhood. It might happen at your engagement party, showers, the rehearsal dinner, or any event during the wedding weekend, or it might be the perfect finish to your perfect wedding reception. Whenever these honored elders stand and ask for everyone's attention, you know something very special is about to pass between you both. These too are words you'll always remember.

Toasts by Parents, Grandparents, Godparents, Guardians, and Just-Like-Parents

"**Nick and Carol,** we wish you both every happiness. We've just been overjoyed at seeing our son so happy and so fulfilled in his life, and Carol, we're so pleased that Nick has won your heart and brought you into our family. We've adored you since the moment we met you, you've been like a daughter to us for a long time now, and we look forward to sharing all the blessings of your future together. We love you both."

"Danielle has always been my Little Sunshine. Nothing makes a grandparent happier than having a new set of little hands to hold, a grandbaby to hug and rock to sleep. Danielle has turned into a beautiful woman as the years have flown by, and she has found her true love. Marvin and I have been married for fifty-two years. I knew he was the one for me by the way he looked at me and winked at me. And when Danielle first introduced Mark to us, I saw that same look in Mark's eye when he looked at Danielle. That's when I knew it was love between them. The good kind of love that lasts forever, because the other person just makes you smile like that. I know that Danielle and Mark have the kind of friendship and love that Marvin and I have for one another. It's so nice to see that in young people today, and it's even better to see that happen for my granddaughter. We know you'll be happy forever, and Danielle, you'll always be my Little Sunshine."

"There's no greater blessing in life than to be a part of a child's life. I've been lucky enough to watch Carrie as she grew from an infant to toddler to a little girl, always amazed by her joy and happiness, her curiosity and her talents, always brightened by her smile and amused by the funny little things she would say. And now I almost can't believe that she's a *bride*. And she is a beautiful bride, as I always knew she would be. Now, it's the greatest blessing to watch her walk off with Ted into the beautiful life she deserves. Sweetie, I wish you and Ted all the best, a lifetime of happiness together and every blessing possible for you."

"Sylvia and I just wanted to take a moment to wish all the greatest love and happiness to Celia and Clay forever and ever, and to officially welcome Clay into our family. And we also welcome Clay's parents, Marcia and Clay Senior, and his brothers and sister, Curtis, Mike, and Melissa into our family as well. As happy as we all are for the bride and groom in their great love story, we are also happy that we get to join with a terrific family that we adore and will share all of Celia and Clay's future joys with. This is a great day for all of us, as our family grows with so much love. To Celia and Clay...and to everyone who loves them. Cheers!"

"We have spent the past twenty-five years wishing and praying for our children's happiness. We've watched them grow into the amazing, strong people they are, and we're so proud to be the parents of such terrific women. And now our youngest daughter's happiness is even greater than we could have wished or prayed for. So we welcome you and we thank you, David, for all you have given to our Lynne, for how happy you make her, for how you support her dreams, for how you wish only the best for her as well…and for how you make it happen for her. We love you both, we will always be here for you, no matter what life brings to your door, and we will always be proud of the two of you."

"**To Jessica and Darren,** who are just starting out on the long journey to forever. Time goes more swiftly than you might think right now. Before you know it, it will be you making a toast at your own child's wedding. May your time together be sweet and savored each and every second."

"**I'd like to propose a toast** to my son, Joey. Son, I can't count the number of times that I have been proud of you. I brag because I'm your father and I'm supposed to do that, but I really do think that God gave me the best son on earth, and I count myself so lucky to have had you all these years. Today, I'm just so proud of you, of the man you've become. You've made your mother and me proud. And you've been my number-one buddy since you were a little guy. So here's to your happiness, to achieving your goals with your beautiful wife by your side."

"**There's a line** in the movie *Father of the Bride* where Steve Martin talks about how a time comes when you have a daughter that you stop worrying about her meeting the wrong guy…and you worry about her meeting the *right* guy. Well, when Dana met Josh, I could tell that he was The Guy. My little girl was going away. I'd be giving her away. I'd be trusting this *Josh guy* with her happiness and her heart. But it didn't take much time before I realized that this *Josh guy* was a decent guy, that he loved her and cared for her and supported her, and that she'd never looked so happy or so beautiful before. I'm a lucky father, and I'm a lucky man. To you, Dana, my little girl, and to you, Josh…To your future together."

Toasts by Siblings

"**Mary,** you're my big sister, and I've spent my life following in your footsteps, following your example, and following your advice. And it's paying off pretty well for me, because I had a lot to aspire to. And now, I'm going to try to follow in your footsteps once again and choose for myself a guy as wonderful as the man you found. I'll aim high like you did. You set the bar pretty high, which only made me a better person. So thank you for being an inspiration to me, for being my friend, and for always being there for me. I'll always be here for you, and I love you very much."

"**Bill,** what can I say? You got the girl. It's been an amazing ride watching you put your life together. And I must admit that some of it has been pretty funny to watch. You started off as this goofy kid who I teased mercilessly and then somewhere you turned into a pretty good guy. Eventually, you became my friend. And now you're my best friend. I might never have said it enough, but I love you and I want you to have all the best things in life that you could ever want. You got the best girl…so now go for the best in everything else. To you."

"**Amy,** my baby sister…you being the bride today means I am getting *old*! But you'll always be my baby sister, the little girl who stole my shoes, tried on my makeup, read my diary, and told more than a few of my early-day boyfriends that they shouldn't kiss me goodnight or they'd die from cooties. You went from being the baby of the family to being the sweetheart of the family, the one we all know we can count on when we need help, the one with the recipes from Grams, the one who's going to find the answer. You were always the one who just wanted to make everyone happy…and now you're so happy yourself. Chris, you know you have a terrific woman in Amy, and we know she's chosen well with you. So here's to your happiness…May you always be sweethearts to one another."

"**Here's to** my terrific big sister…no matter where our lives may lead us, we both know that we'll always have each other because the bond between us cannot be broken by any distance. You've been a part of my life for my whole life…you've taught me just about everything I know in the important worlds of fashion, business, movies, art, and music and you supported me in my career when everyone else questioned what I was doing. It was you saying, 'I believe in you' that nudged me on the road to my brand of happiness, and now I'm very happy to get to see you off into yours. You're a part of my heart, and I'll love you always."

Toasts to Friends and Family

Friends are the family of the heart. This section is devoted to paying tribute to the women who are like sisters to you and the men who are your brothers from another mother. They could be cousins who are more like friends, even a sister or brother you count among your friends. Friends come in all varieties, and they can be longer lasting than some of the really good furniture you own.

Without them, then, this wedding day wouldn't be happening at all. (And if you're *not* the bride or groom reading this book, the friend in question could be the guest of honor!)

So pay tribute to them now, for all they bring to you, and for the never-ending bond you'll have into the future.

Quotes About Friends

"Friendship is the source of the greatest pleasures, and without friends even the most agreeable of pursuits becomes tedious."
—St. Thomas Aquinas

"Friends are the sunshine of life."

—John Hay

"My best friend is the one who brings out the best in me."

—Henry Ford

"Friends show their love in times of trouble."

—Euripides

"Only equals can be friends."

—Maya Angelou

"A true friend is one soul in two bodies."

—Aristotle

"Fate chooses our relatives, we choose our friends."

—Jacques Delille

"It's so clear that you have to cherish everyone."

—Alice Walker

"The greatest sweetener of life is friendship."

—Joseph Addison

"A true friend is somebody who can make us do what we can."

—Ralph Waldo Emerson

"A friend is someone who gives you total freedom to be yourself."

—Jim Morrison

"A man's friendships are one of the best measures of his worth."

—Charles Darwin

"A friend is, as it were, a second self."

—Cicero

"Friendship is a sheltering tree."

—Samuel Taylor Coleridge

"The world is round so that friendship can encircle it."

—Pierre Teilhard De Chardin

"A faithful friend is a strong defense, and he that hath found one hath found a treasure."

—Ecclesiastes 6:14

"Friendship is love without its wings."

—Lord Byron

"Don't walk in front of me, I may not follow; Don't walk behind me, I may not lead; Just walk beside me and be my friend."

—Albert Camus

"Dina, I wanted to thank you for flying halfway across the world to be with me here today. You'll never know how much I appreciate that, because my wedding day would have had a little chunk missing from it if my best friend were not here to share it with me. So thank you for always being the true and genuine friend that you are, for making it effortless to know you, and for making my day into complete perfection just by your being here. I love you, sweetie!"

"Genevieve, several years ago you helped set me on a course that was going to change my life incredibly and permanently. When you asked me to spend the summer out in Switzerland with you and with your family, I jumped at the chance to romp around Europe with my closest friend and her family that's like family to me. And there we were waiting for the lift on Mt. Pilatus when up walked a handsome, blonde man with what seemed to be a broken ankle. We helped him down the mountain, and you were intuitive enough to know to leave me there to tend to him. And now he and I are married. If it weren't for you and for our Swiss winter adventure, Nicolas's and my paths would never have crossed. So this toast is for you, and for the amazing way the fates work. One great friendship led to one great trip, which led to one great love. We both thank you and your family, for the adventure of it all, and for being such a big part of our hearts."

"**Casey and Tina,** when you first told me you wanted to set me up on a blind date, I thought I'd rather get my legs waxed than go through another brutal first meeting. But you surprised me by choosing the most amazing man I'd ever met. As some of you might know, that date went so well, it didn't end for about nine hours. Casey and Tina, you know me well and you knew the wishes of my heart, and you delivered the man of my dreams. So thank you from my very wish-fulfilled heart for taking the chance, for working to convince me to take a risk, and for putting both of our lives on a new path toward happiness. We love you both and this day is partially because of you."

"**Fawn, Heidi, and Lisa,** we've been through so much of life together. All the best days of my teenage and college years have you as a part of every memory. It makes me so happy to have you here to stand up with me and to be my bridesmaids. All I am today came about during our shared years, all the experiences we helped each other through, all the lessons we learned from one another. None of us are complete without the others—we're a package deal. Luckily, Kent is aware of this! Friendship lasts forever, and I know that when I'm old and Botoxed and still looking fabulous we will still have one another and margaritas and Ben and Jerry's on girls' nights out. We keep each other young and laughing, we never let anything stop us, and we allow each other to dream big. It's true friendship, the greatest gift. I love you all."

"Susan, thank you so much for being my partner in crime, for taking this shy little bookworm ten years ago and bringing me out into a world of excitement and travel and adventure. You opened up doors to me that I didn't even know to knock on. You did more to expand my horizons in just a few months and you got me to ask myself many soul-defining questions. I believe that people can be great teachers, that you meet people for a reason, and I know that our friendship came about to open up new worlds to me. Now here I am with a great big door open for me, and I'm so excited to have you here to watch me leap through. Thank you, thank you, thank you for saying 'you can do it.' Now I know I can do anything."

"True friends know you better than you know yourself. And with Carrie and Lila, I know that's true. They knew I was in love with Todd before I knew. They teased me relentlessly and better yet…they never let me doubt myself or doubt his love for me. With them cheering me on, I opened my heart to Todd and eventually threw away any fears that might have hurt our relationship. So I'd like to drink to you, my very best friends, for giving me the gift of a lifetime, for cheering me on, and for wishing better for me than I dared to wish for myself. I love you both more than I can describe, and I believe in *you* and in your happiness for the future."

"**Jeff,** you're not only my brother, you're my best friend. From our youngest days, I protected you and you defended me. I helped you learn the finer points of picking up women, and you helped me learn the finer points of being a good man. I helped you with your career, and you helped me plan my life. We've been partners not just in the family but also in the world. I'm lucky to have you as my little brother and I'll always be here for you, buddy."

"**Jason, Joey, Big T, and Randy…**we started off as little hellions, we worried our mothers sick with our BB gun fights and our motorcycles and all those broken bones. We were the epitome of 'boys will be boys.' I'll always remember those days. Then, one by one, we started losing the bad boy thing. We each found the love of a good woman and wanted to better ourselves so they would have us. If anyone here could have heard that coming about, it probably would be pretty funny to hear. Big T once came to me and asked me how to make *tiramisu*. I knew it was all over then. Our hellion days were done and gone.

So the former hellion boys started asking the big questions...'How can I win her over?' 'How can I be good enough *for her?*' 'What do women really want?' Eventually, we all found our way and found the answers and we helped each other become real men, real gentlemen, men of substance. We helped each other grow up...much to our mothers' relief. Guys, thank you for giving me that golden childhood of carefree days and fearless adventures, really dumb moves, and really great recoveries. You're my brothers, and you always will be."

"Everyone, this is George, our boss. I just wanted to thank George for transferring me out of accounts receivable so that I could date someone at the office without setting off corporate alarm bells. I had an agenda—to date Pam—and George knew it. And he put my transfer into the works so that I could go after the woman of my dreams. So George, here's to you and to your small but pivotal part in our success story."

"To all of our friends, near and far, those who could travel to be here with us tonight, and those who couldn't but are with us in their hearts and best wishes. We're blessed to have such an incredible, dynamic, and diverse group of special people in our lives whom we call friends. Our lives are richer because of all of you, we're grateful to know you and for all of the gifts you give us every day. We'll be here always for each and every one of you, so here's to you and to the happiness of your lives!"

12

Toasts in Remembrance

Weddings can be bittersweet events when a parent, a sibling, a grandparent, friend, or other loved one is missing from the picture. I've spoken with recent brides whose mothers or fathers had passed away and were not there to either help them into a gown or walk them down the aisle—important family moments the bride has dreamed about all her life. Missing that loved one on such a momentous, sentimental day can bring tears or just a slight hollow feeling when *I wish my Dad was here* creeps through the excitement of the wedding day and casts a light mist of sorrow. The brides I spoke to said they knew their parent would be there in spirit, and they wished to pay tribute to that departed family member during the ceremony with a candle lighting, a dedication of the floral arrangements in that person's memory, or during the reception with a toast.

This is where you come in. The words you speak in remembrance of *any* departed, adored family member adds an incredible touch of sentimentality to the wedding day. Even though guests, or the bride and groom, might get teary-eyed at this tribute, you've contributed a very valuable personalization to the couple's big day. And you're giving them something priceless: including the loved one in their wedding, which will certainly touch all hearts and memories.

Here, then, are several examples you might consider for a remembrance toast to a loved one:

"If I could just take a moment to ask everyone to lift their glasses...As many of you might know, Deborah's father Mike passed away last year. While he's greatly missed on this day by all of us, he is most assuredly here with us in spirit to watch his daughter get married. Mike was extremely proud of Deborah, as he was of all of his kids and grandkids, and if he were here right now, I'm sure he'd say how beautiful Deborah looks, how proud he is of all she's become and accomplished, and how happy he is that she found a wonderful man to share her life with. He was a very proud father, he loved his family more than life itself, and he did a wonderful job raising his daughters to be the incredible women they are. Here's to Mike...Always in our hearts."

"Some of you here might not have had the blessing of knowing the bride's grandmother Sophia, whom we lost six years ago and miss greatly. Sophia was the quintessential grandmother, always ready with a hug or a present for the kids, always cooking up something amazing in her kitchen, always with the perfect, common sense words of wisdom any of us needed. She taught Stacy her recipes, her gardening skills, and from what I hear a few racy jokes as well. Sophia was a wonderful soul, a kind and gentle spirit, nurturing to her very core, just radiating love for her family and many friends. We know she's watching over Stacy, Matt, and all of us right now, probably with a few things to say about the marinara sauce and meatballs, as much a part of today as any of us are. Sophia's favorite drink was a White Russian, so as I'm sure you see, Stacy and Matt have instructed the servers to place a snifter of Sophia's favorite drink by each of your place settings. Please join me now in raising that glass in Sophia's memory, as we all think of our favorite memories with her, and drink to her everlasting peace. She lived well, she laughed often, she loved much. To Sophia!"

"I'd like to propose a toast...to the memory of all of our departed loved ones and friends who could not be with us to share in Sam and Dana's big day. You are in our hearts forever."

"Here's to the memories we all share of several special people we all wish could be here with us today...Jeff's father Jason and his grandfather George, Anna's grandparents Lincoln and Annabella, and Kimberly and Marshall, friends of the bride and groom who perished on September 11, 2001. Wherever you are, we know you're watching over your loved ones from afar, and we keep you in our hearts, minds and prayers. We miss you, and we are all better people for having known you as long as we were blessed to do so."

DEDICATING A SONG IN THE LOVED ONE'S MEMORY

"As you all know, Nancy's mother has left us all too soon and is missed more than words can express, especially on this day. Nancy thought it would be wonderful for us all to remember her mom this evening during a dance to her mother's favorite song, the song she always requested at weddings, the song she'd dance to by herself in the kitchen on summer nights, the song she danced to with her children when they were babies: 'What a Wonderful World,' by Louis Armstrong. So everyone please join us on the dance floor and remember Nancy's mother, the very graceful and very beautiful Noreen."

13

Toasts for Children

Weddings are all about family, and the kids bring warmth, laughter, and innocence to the party...*or* they bring a very amusing tantrum right in the middle of the dance floor during the cake-cutting ceremony, much to their parents' dismay. Whatever the demeanors of the little ones, the kids are the bright, new little branch of the family tree and might just as well be honored with a tribute.

For instance, a bride and groom with kids of their own might take this time to address their sons and daughters in a much more detailed and sentimental speech than they were afforded during the simple vows they took as a blending family during the ceremony. If it was the gentle way the groom behaved with his goddaughter that made the bride fall in love with him when they first met—and know that he would be a great father himself someday—the bride can touch hearts by thanking the little girl for being such a special part of the groom's life and teaching him about unconditional love.

Or, an adorable collection of little girls in their pink flower girl dresses, pre-teen junior bridesmaids, and the little guy in the pint-sized cummerbund and matching bow tie can step bravely forward to propose a thank-you toast of their own to their parents (coached from the sidelines by a helpful bridesmaid or grandmother). Now *this* is an unforgettable moment at the wedding...the kids standing up to say a few precious words in a short script *or performing* a little something for the guests of honor. At some weddings, the kids step into the spotlight to recite a rehearsed poem or do their little dance from dancing school to big applause, and their childlike need for attention is satiated for the rest of the evening. Little ones might not be able to recite Shakespearean sonnets, but they can do a mean Eensy Weensy Spider as code for "Thank you and I love you."

Here are some ideas for toasts to and from the children of the wedding day:

Toasts To Children

One hint on proposing toasts to kids...keep them short. Sometimes kids get embarrassed when a parent hugs them in public or says "I love you" in public, so depending on the child's age and comfort with mushiness, spare the child potential squirms and make it short and sweet.

"I'd like to propose a toast to Mattie and Ken, who have been the light of my life. Kids, I love you and will always love you."

"Tara, Elaina, and Mitch, you're such special kids, and I'm very happy that I get to spend my life being there for you as well as for your mother. I never thought I could be so lucky as to have a beautiful new wife like your mother and three smart, great kids like you to care for as well."

"**Jessie,** our baby, we know you're not old enough to understand quite what's going on, and someday you'll look at the videotape of today and you'll get it. We're so blessed to have our little angel be with us on our wedding day. It wouldn't be half as special without you. We love you, you're a joy in our lives, and we can't wait to see what the future brings to all of us, especially to you."

"**Cara and Ryan,** I wanted to take a moment to thank you both for opening your hearts to me and welcoming me into your family way back when...letting me into your lives and showing me who you are and how well you love your mother. I love her more because of how much she loves you. You could have made it hard on me to win her heart, but you didn't. And thanks for not making it hard for me to win your hearts...You have won mine. I'll always, always be here for you."

"**Jada and Jordan,** Casey and Emily, we're so proud of the family we are. We may have made it official today, but you have been sisters and we your parents for a long time now. This is the best day of our lives, partly because you are here and because we get to give you the gift of each other and of ourselves as your adoring parents. Nothing has made us happier than seeing you all grow closer to one another and act like true sisters—including the fights over the curling iron—and to hear the sounds of your laughter throughout the house. We're blessed to have you in our lives, and we love you very much."

If you're into public displays of adoration, now is a good time to give the kids a special gift from you— a diamond pendant, a silver heart locket, a bracelet, something to make the moment extra special.

"Emma and Ashley, we'd like to give you a little something from both of us. Since you *are* our hearts, we give you these heart lockets to wear and to remember always the happiness you bring us and how much we love you."

"Emma and Ashley, you are priceless gems to your mother and to me, so we give you these special gifts as a token of our love for you. Wear them in good health, in happiness and to always remember this day. We love you."

Toasts By Children
If the kids love the spotlight, and—whether coached or not by an adult—they want to take the floor to wish the happy couple happiness, here are some sample toasts for children to make...

From the tiny ones...
"Here's to Mommy and Ethan...from me."
"I want to make a toast...to my daddy and to Trisha: Happy wedding day! I love you."

This Song Is for You...

Again, you might skip the verbal mushiness and just dedicate a song to them...sometimes kids are more comfortable hearing a pop star talk about love than if those words came from their parents. Plus, bringing the kids out on the dance floor can make for picture-perfect memories for all of you...provided the kids aren't in their shy pre-teens where a singled-out dance with their mom and stepdad in front of everyone would be social torture. It might be best to just dedicate the song to them and let everyone enjoy it on the dance floor along with you. The photographer can still capture the smiles on your happy family's faces as you join hands and sing out loud, as you twirl one another or as you both hold the children in your arms.

From the school-agers...

"I love you, Mommy and Ethan. I'm happy that this is your wedding day, and that you are happy."

"For Daddy and Trisha...Kelsey and I wanted to say thank you for being so good to us and for giving us the necklaces. We love you."

"Happy wedding, Mommy and Ethan! Kelsey and I wrote a poem for you...

'Mommy's the bride,

Ethan's the groom,

Now that we're moving,

Can we have a bigger room?

Mommy looks happy,

Ethan looks glad,

And now with our new Daddy,

No one will be sad.'
That's it."

Now's the ideal time for kids to steal hearts—and not just the spotlight—with the presentation of a gift to the happy couple...

"Kelsey and I made something for Daddy and Trisha...Actually, Grandma helped us...(*unwrapping gift*) It's a picture of Daddy, Trisha, Kelsey and me at the zoo when we first met Trisha, before Daddy and Trisha were in love. Grandma said it would be nice to give you this today, so Kelsey and I took the picture from the album and we made the frame for you. We hope you like it."

Teenagers
Teenagers and young adults can recite any well-wishing toast, dedicate a song, give a gift, open with a joke, or share a personal anecdote about the bride and groom. Many teenaged kids of the bride or groom often joke about the hard time they gave their parent's "new date" the first time he or she met them, and how they made their parent's significant other jump through some hoops before they embraced them. Teens can possess a sharp sense of wit, and they often deliver toasts that are laced with popular culture and big laughs. When things get sentimental, that's an important bonding moment between parent and child as "the child" moves into adulthood. Here's an example:

"**Here's to my dad** and Trisha—congratulations on your wedding. I wanted to take a few minutes to share a story with you. The night that Dad first met Trisha, I knew when he came home that night that he was really gone over her. He had this goofy grin on his face, he asked me right then to help him pick out a shirt for their next date...which was going to be a week later. Oh, yeah, he was gone over her. The best was when I caught him dancing in front of the mirror when he thought no one was looking. Trisha was taking him out salsa dancing for one of their dates, so Dad put on Telemundo and was salsa-ing by himself in his boxer shorts. Any woman who can make my dad *dance* has to be something special. So we met Trisha...and we liked her immediately. We loved how my dad just lit up when she was around, how he looked ten years younger just from talking about her, how she brought out this romantic guy in him. We'd never seen Dad like that, and we must admit it was pretty funny. Especially the boxer shorts episode. But it's all because Trisha is such an amazing woman. I hope I meet a woman someday who's just like her, and then I'll be the one dancing around in my underwear. Dad, Trisha, I'm so happy that you found each other, that you clicked like you did, that you make each other laugh, and that you're parents we can trust and go to no matter what. I love you both, and I wish you all the best. Trisha, welcome to the family, and Dad...we love you."

Part Three:

Specialty Wedding Toasts

14

Second Weddings

As with any second wedding in its entirety, some-times the couple chooses *not* to make any reference that either of them have been married before. Their wedding day, for them, is not a time for looking backwards at where they've been and with whom they once shared a walk down the aisle...but rather for looking *forward* to a life with their present love. That said, if you're making a toast at a second wedding, you'll really need to weigh the situation and choose your words gracefully. It might be that you know the bride doesn't want any mention of her first marriage at all—to her, it never happened. Or it might be that the bride's family is just getting over their initial hesitancy about the groom's previous marriage, so it's best not to open old wounds. Whatever the case, you know the situation best—pick your wedding toast words with thought toward the diplomacy of it all. Subtlety is best. Make passing reference to a life's First Act without being specific.

Here, then, are some sample toasts that can be suitable at a second wedding where it's fine to refer to the couple's history...

"They say that 'good things come to those who

wait.' For Jenny and Steve, that is so true. The wait was long, and at times difficult, then fulfilling and then full of hope. And now we're all here today to celebrate with them the good that came to them after all this time. Jenny and Steve, here's to your happiness, well-deserved and well-timed, for all eternity."

"In the movie *The Natural*, Glenn Close's character says something along the lines of 'You live two lives: one you learn from, and the other you live.' Jenny and Steve arrived at this day ready to live their wonderful life together, carrying with them all they've learned in their pasts. They bring with them great knowledge and wisdom, great love of their families and friends, and great love for one another. Jenny and Steve, you've been preparing for this wedding day for, what? A year? But you've been preparing to be with one another all of your lives. We stand here with you to wish you all that's good in life, years of happiness together, and a partnership that's just...natural. Here's to you!"

"Those of us who have known Jenny and Steve for a long time know the roads they've each traveled up to this point. We've cheered them on their high roads, comforted them on their low roads, we've pulled them from the side of the road on occasion—OK, I'll stop with the 'roads' analogy...for now. We've all loved Jenny and Steve for so long, and this is a happy day for all of us as well, to see them so happy and so in love, to see where the road has taken them perfectly so they could meet one another, knowing that every twist and turn and detour was meant to be, to get them to right now. So here's to you, Jenny and Steve...May this be the start of a whole new exciting journey with just the right twists and turns along the way to make the ride exciting and always to deliver you exactly where you need to be. With each other."

"To Jenny and Steve...A better partnership never existed before this day, and I know I speak for everyone when I say how happy we all are that these two incredible people found one another in this crowded world, took a chance on love, and opened their hearts for the greatest blessing anyone could ever ask for...a happy marriage. We wish them all the best that life has to offer, a lifetime full of love, laughter, joy, and comfort, and good friends and family to share it with. To Jenny and Steve!"

"If anyone out there still believes that true love is a fairy tale, that wishes and dreams only come true in the movies, and that romance is a thing of the past...just look at Jenny and Steve. Look at the smiles on their faces, how beautiful Jenny looks today, and how Steve can't hide the fact that he's the luckiest man in the world. Dreams do come true, even after long waits and sleepless nights, even after first, second, or a hundred attempts at happiness. When it's right, it's perfection. So here's to Jenny and Steve—May you continue to dream your dreams, may all your dreams come true, and may everyone you meet be inspired by you...I know we all are."

"They say love is lovelier the second time

around. We can all see how lovely Jenny looks, how loved Jenny and Steve are by everyone in this room, and just how much they love each other. We wish you both the best of everything and a life filled with love that gets lovelier every day. Here's to you!"

"As I stand here and look at Jenny and Steve, I can't help but think, isn't life funny? It's not ours to wonder why our lives move us around the way they do, but rather to be thankful that they move us to the places where we stand. I stand here now, looking at Jenny and Steve, thrilled for their happiness, proud to call them my friends, and excited to see where life takes them next."

"To Jenny and Steve as they start a new chapter in the book of their lives. There may have been parts that made them laugh or cry, but no doubt this is a love story with a happy beginning...with no ending in sight. Here's to the story you'll write together...Cheers!"

"Not too long ago, I think I can safely say that neither Jenny nor Steve thought they'd find themselves here, in love, getting married, looking toward a future together. As Jenny's friend, I knew a time when she thought love might never come again. But as I told her, 'never say never.' And now I can say, 'I told you so!' Jenny might have been a little surprised when love arrived and Steve might have been nervous to love again as well, but no one who knows either of them is surprised at all because we know what amazing, lovable people they are...how strong and faith-filled, courageous, generous, and kind as individuals. And when these two came together, we all said, 'Of course! They're perfect together!' Some of us may have known they were perfect together before they did and we watched as silent (or not so silent) observers as they both just started to glow and smile and laugh more, as the word 'we' crept into their conversations, and as we could never get Jenny or Steve on the phone anymore. It was love. Not surprising, not at all. Jenny and Steve are perfect for one another. They complement each other, bring out the best in one another, endure the worst in one another with a smile, and forgive one another. We've all seen these two people blossom and open up more beautifully than they ever have before, because it's so right between them. It's just a beautiful thing. Jenny, Steve, I wish you all the best that life can give, all the love in the world, and your every dream come true. I love you both. Here's to you!"

"Jenny and Steve are amazing people as individuals, but they're even more amazing together. They've each found their other half...at last. You can never wait too long for true love, and luckily for Jenny and Steve, the wait wasn't too long. But it was worth it, right? So before another minute goes by, let's toast the beautiful bride and her very lucky groom...and invite them back out onto the dance floor for a song that I'm dedicating to them now...'At Last,' by Etta James."

Say It in a Song

Sometimes, the words of a song just capture the emotion of a second wedding, so you might want to keep your own words brief, let the song do the talking, and give the bride and groom something priceless: the enduring memory of a dance to a song you chose for them. I absolutely love "At Last" by Etta James for this particular type of wedding. It's perfection. Some other songs you might consider are "True Love," by Elton John and Kiki Dee; "I Cross My Heart," by George Strait; "The Way You Look Tonight," by Frank Sinatra; "It Had to Be You," by Harry Connick Jr.; and "True Colors," by Cyndi Lauper or Phil Collins. Choose any song that fits your bride and groom's story, and give them a second "our song" to remember forever.

INCLUDING KIDS AND STEP-KIDS IN THE TOAST

"**Jenny and Steve** have never looked happier. They've won the happiness lottery in finding each other after all this time and in creating a family and a happy home. What more could anyone ask for? So please join me in toasting the new Mr. and Mrs. Steve Jones, and their children Miles, Melissa, and Emily…may every happiness be yours today, tomorrow, and forever. Cheers!"

"**This is a very happy day.** Jenny and Steve become husband and wife, Miles, Melissa, and Emily gain a new stepmom, and we all get to share in this moment with you. We wish you a lifetime of love in the family you have now become. We wish you a lifetime of laughter—may you always make each other smile and find yourselves smiling when you think of how blessed you are. We wish you a lifetime of faith—faith in one another, in yourselves, and in those who adore you. We wish you a lifetime of generosity—may you always give to one another and receive from one another. We wish you a lifetime of lessons—that you may teach and learn from one another's triumphs and mistakes. We wish you a lifetime of hands to hold, loved ones to hug, dreams to realize, hopes to share, and a place and people to always call home. Here's to you, Jenny, Steve, and the kids...we wish you a lifetime of joy."

"Please lift your glasses in a toast to Jenny, Steve, Miles, Melissa, and Emily—may the love you share as a happy family only grow stronger by the minute. We've watched as you all came together, as you grew to love one another, and as you took your vows as a family today. We love you, and we will always be there for you. Cheers!"

15

Destination Weddings

When a wedding has transported the bride, groom, and all their guests to an exotic island, foreign city, or ski resort, this unique celebration welcomes a unique twist to personalizing the toast. Everyone in attendance has not just one thing in common—loving the bride and groom—but now a *second:* they've come on a romantic journey to join them as they wed. Your speech unites the two for an all-inclusive toast to remember...

"Helen Keller has been quoted as saying 'Life is either a daring adventure or nothing at all.' What we all love about Sarah and Tom is their love of adventure, and I speak for everyone when I say thank you for inviting us all here to this beautiful island to share this adventure with you. I know we all love seeing the sunset, the scuba diving, the gorgeous rooms by the beach, and time for romance of our own—but by far the most beautiful and romantic thing we've seen yet is watching Sarah and Tom together. No sunset can compete with that kind of inspiring beauty. I wish you both a lifetime of shared sunsets, and all the adventure and beauty your life can hold. To your future!"

"Knowing Sarah and Tom's love for each other, I know they'd both go to the ends of the earth to be together...and they've brought us along. They'd swim across the seas to be together...and they've brought us along. They'd cross the sky to be together...and they've brought us along. Thank you, Sarah and Tom, for inviting us to paradise. Thank you for the gift of your friendship all these years. *That* is the most beautiful thing we've seen here in paradise—the love you share for each other and with all of us. So here's to your love and happiness, to your every romantic, adventurous, exotic, and inspiring moment from now on. Aloha, and congratulations!"

"Let me start off by saying, Wow! Sarah and Tom, you really know how to make a special moment unforgettable. I think we've all seen some amazing things here in Paris...legendary art masterpieces, the view from the top of the Eiffel Tower, incredible meals and great wine, a Hermès scarf I'm going back to buy tomorrow. It's no wonder that the most romantic couple I've ever met would marry here in Paris...I know your dreams have come true: marrying here, marrying each other, and having all of us here to share it with you. You might not ask for more, but we all wish you even more in life than this dream come true. May this be only the start of your travels and adventures together. May this be the first of many masterpieces in your life. May you fill your lives with endless chances for romance and shared joys, across the world and in your own home, for all the days of your life. *Je t'aime* Sarah, *Je t'aime* Tom, *Je t'aime toujours.*"

[Translation of French: "I love you Sarah, I love you Tom, I love you always."]

"It's not the destination but the journey that matters most. For Sarah and Tom, the journey is underway. It has been since the first day they met. The journey is day after day of love and excitement, adventure, once-in-a-lifetime moments, new sights, sounds, and tastes, lessons and unforgettable memories, and a dear one's hand to hold along the way. Sarah and Tom, may you always hold each other's hands as you set off into the journey of a lifetime. To you! And to love!"

"Okay, this just in…we got the whole time zone thing confused, and Sarah and Tom are not supposed to be married until tomorrow! Just kidding! I might not know what day it is, but I do know that this is indeed a wonderful day. Sarah and Tom, my sister and my friend, are now married. Here's to your everlasting happiness and harmony. No matter what time zone you find yourselves in, may you always be Home to each other."

16

Outdoor Weddings

Outdoor weddings are growing more and more popular as brides and grooms fulfill their dreams of marrying on the beach, in a botanical garden, on a yacht, or even in their own backyards. There's something magical about weddings that take place under the sun or stars—perhaps it calls back to the days of Olde English wedding celebrations in village squares, processions through the streets of Italy, Shakespearean and Jane Austen scenes of great romantic love stories come to a happy ending. Or maybe it's Brad Pitt and Jennifer Aniston's outdoor wedding that's inspiring everyone to hold an outdoor wedding these days.

Whatever the reason, and whatever planning the bride and groom went through to set up their elaborate tents and tables and silk-backed chairs, rose-covered trellises, fountains lit with glowing sapphire lights, a canopy of trees defining the path to the aisle...an outdoor wedding is beautiful by nature. So the nature of your wedding toast can tie in the theme of the outdoors, the beauty of the surroundings, or the couple's love of everything oceanic. Here are just a few samples to get you thinking *outside* the usual realm of wedding toasts and in an out-doors theme:

"Here's to you as the sun sets on your single life and the moon rises to greet you as a newly married couple. May the sun always shine on you, and may the moon always see you gently off to sleep, for each and every day of your happy life together."

"To Kelly and Mark...here's to a life of beauty inside and out. Here's to sunny skies and warm summer breezes—to a perfect day in all aspects of the word. You deserve nothing less than the best, and you have it in one another. To your happiness!"

"We all know that Mark proposed to Kelly on the beach right here in Cape Cod last summer, so it fits perfectly that they should marry here. I know Kelly has loved coming here to the Cape with her family every summer. She has wonderful memories here with her sisters, with her friends, and with her grandparents, whom she misses very much. This place has a part of her heart. So it's only natural that she should meet the man of her dreams right here four years ago during one of her summer road trips with the girls. This place that has her heart gave her the gift of her husband. Mark proposed to Kelly right here where we're standing now, and she said yes. So we all gather here for the happy couple and we watch both their hearts fill with joy and happiness and the promise of love everlasting. And it fills our hearts as well. Now we all have a great love memory here at the Cape. And Kelly and Mark will return here summer after summer to visit the spot where it all began...and then all *really* began for them. And someday they'll be one of those blissfully happy elderly couples who stroll hand-in-hand on the beach without a care in the world, with their hands fitting together so well you can't tell whose fingers are whose. Kelly always said she wished she could have a love and a romance like that some day, and now she has it. She and Mark have it. We wish you every happiness and a lifetime of walks on the beach. To Kelly and Mark!"

"It's a beautiful night, isn't it? The moon is bright, the stars are out...It's all just perfection out there. As it is right here, right now for Kelly and Mark. May your love last a day for every star up in the heavens, and may your every wish come true."

"Some of you might notice the flowers in your centerpieces. They're gardenias, Kelly's favorite flower. The gardenia was her grandmother's favorite flower as well. And Kelly always knew—before she knew who her husband would be—that she would have gardenias at her wedding. When Kelly was a little girl, she and her grandmother would spend hours out in the garden, cutting peace roses, planting daffodil bulbs in the fall, staking the tomatoes. She got from her grandmother a love of all things in the garden, and now her wedding in this botanical garden is like heaven to her. Some of you might know that Kelly knew Mark was The One when he started making flowers a part of his courtship. On date number one, he brought her yellow tulips. Very romantic, Mark.

On date number four, he took her to the Philadelphia Flower Show. Big points, Mark. Big points. But it wasn't until he brought her a gardenia—not even knowing how much gardenias mean to her—that Kelly started glancing at bridal magazines and walking a little more slowly past the windows of jewelry stores. Mark knows what makes Kelly's heart soar, which is what makes him so perfect for her. Kelly and Mark, may your love blossom forever and grow and multiply and beautify your world for all the days of your lives. Congratulations!"

"**Mother Nature** gave Kelly and Mark a beautiful day, didn't she? The sun is shining, the rain this morning made us all nervous, but it cleared up in time to make everything bright and beautiful for the wedding. 'Into each life a little rain must fall,' they say. So remember this, Kelly and Mark...love each other during times of sunshine, and love each other during times of rainfall, for the rain makes everything new and bright and beautiful again. You are blessed in having one another, and we are all blessed in having you in our lives as well. Here's to a lifetime of bright and beautiful blessings!"

"**Please join me** in raising your glasses to the new Mr. and Mrs. Mark Stevens. They've known each other since they were in the second grade. Mark used to pull Kelly's pigtails on the playground, and they spent much of their childhood playing right here in this backyard with all the other neighborhood kids. They camped out in the treehouse, they made mud pies, they organized lemonade stands. Just all the great snapshots of childhood innocence that we smile to ourselves over when we see them out the kitchen window. That little girl and that little boy grew up, fell in love, and now they've married right here at home, in the same yard of their childhood dreams and schemes. Now, they have new dreams and schemes together, and they have 122 of their closest friends and family here to wish them well, to love them and smile at this priceless snapshot of true love and dreams come true. Kelly and Mark, this will always be your home, even as you build your own new one. I love you both, and I wish you all the greatest dreams of your childhood, your adulthood and your future together all come true. To your happiness!"

17

Post-Elopement Celebrations

Sometimes the wedding couple just takes off and gets married without all the fanfare of planning a big wedding. They might have escaped the pressures of wedding stress by jetting out to Vegas on the spur of the moment, or they might have always planned to marry simply and quietly, perhaps on a beach in Hawaii—and send a postcard to the folks back home. For some, the huge $50,000 expense and a full year of hectic work to plan a full-blown elegant wedding are *not* their idea of a romantic fantasy. It's better just to elope, tie the knot together as they feel it should be done, and then celebrate the good news with everyone back home at a later date.

These post-elopement receptions are obviously a way for the couple to enjoy the company of their family and friends without obligating *anyone* to pay for a bridesmaid's dress, or a bridal shower, or (especially for parents) the immense cost of a wedding production. It's just all about spending quality time with loved ones and soaking in the shared joys of togetherness, embracing, laughing, sharing stories…formally at a dinner, informally at a barbecue, or just over cake and coffee.

Where you come in is tailoring your toast—and there *should* definitely be toasts at this great family occasion!—to capture the mood and tone and persona of the celebration itself. Delayed or not, it's very special to the couple to toast and be toasted after an elopement…perhaps slightly more so than couples at traditional weddings. Now is their time to share their happiness with their favorite people, one of them being you. So consider the following possibilities for a post-elopement toast:

"Beth and Tony, when you married in Belize, know that we were all right there with you. We're a part of you, so if you're there, we're there too. And we'll always be with you wherever you go, because love doesn't need physical presence—love is just with you all the time. Family and friends are a part of your heart, and you are a part of ours. So we're proud and pleased and thrilled to be here with you now, to celebrate your marriage, to wish you all of life's blessings, and to let you know just how much we love you. Congratulations!"

"Beth and Tony, we're so happy to share this night with you in celebration of the best day of your lives and the best news we've heard in a long time. Congratulations on your marriage, and here's to a long and happy life together!"

"With Beth and Tony, it's always been about love, about happiness, generosity, kindness, and fun.

They have their priorities in line, and they always do right by one another. Now, they've done it right again. It wasn't about a big wedding with all the trimmings. For them, it was about the *marriage*, about joining their lives together forever. That's the most important part that so many others out there seem to forget when they're fighting about napkin colors and icing flavors. It's about the *marriage*. And we celebrate that tonight, all together here to honor you, Beth and Tony, to share your great news, and to wish you every happiness life has to offer."

"Let's drink a toast to Mr. and Mrs. Tony Abbott. Their rings may have already found a home on their fingers, the top layer of their wedding cake may already be in their freezer, but they're still on their honeymoon and it's never too late—or too often—for all of their loved ones to come together in celebration of the giant leap of full faith they've taken. We're so pleased, so thrilled to share this evening with you, to see you so much in love, and to give you another big day to remember forever. Here's to your marriage—may it be forever strong."

"Is anyone here surprised that Tony and Beth eloped? They've always been spontaneous and adventurous, always full of surprises. Their second date was a weekend trip to Tahoe...and they came back six days later. Beth moved across the country to follow her passion, and Tony quit his job to follow her there. A good marriage and a strong love is all about taking risks, taking leaps, forgetting about fear, and following your heart, following your passions. Tony and Beth have all of those qualities, which makes us love them even more...and probably even want to be more like them sometimes. They're the perfect pair, so alike in all that they do, and I'm sure they'll be surprising one another and all of us as well for all the days of their lives. The best of everything to you! May you live your life together with passion, without boundaries, and with full faith...forever."

Since post-elopement parties are often more informal, more intimate and more laid back than traditional weddings, a good dose of humor is often called for...

"Everyone please join me in lifting your glasses to Tony and Beth. You've given each other a priceless gift when you joined your lives in marriage. And you've given us a priceless gift as well...nobody here, and I mean nobody, will have to dance the chicken dance, the hokey pokey, the Macarena, or any other stupid line dance tonight! So here's to Tony and Beth for sparing us the humiliation, the awkwardness, the way-too-enthusiastic deejay, and the reminder of this family's congenital lack of rhythm. Congratulations on your marriage, kids! Here's to your happiness and your partnership, together forever. We love you! Cheers!"

Toasts of Advice

A great wedding toast isn't just about telling the bride and groom you love them, that you wish them happiness and dreams come true. It isn't just about making them laugh or cry. It can also be a poignant moment when you give the happy couple some meaningful advice about how to make their marriage work. Remember, this is the best day of their lives, but it's also the *first* day of their marriage. And every bride and groom steps out of the limousine believing that their partnership will stand the test of time. Your words of instruction can start them off to a better chance at forever together.

Perhaps you've been married for thirty years to your high school sweetheart. Your words of wisdom, then, are most definitely welcome. Anyone who loves and loves well, who has one of the keys to a happy marriage—whether happily married themselves or not—is welcome to share some of their sage advice as a gift to the newlyweds. Every bit of insight helps in this world of ours where frozen pizzas have a longer shelf life than some marriages. So to help the bride and groom into their happily ever after, you might choose to deliver some thoughts like the following:

* Remember that you're friends first and spouses second.
* Make time to laugh together.
* Never go to bed angry.
* Listen, really listen to one another.
* Allow one another some bad days...grant each other the peace of knowing you can both be human.
* Love one another for your faults as well as your strengths.
* Always speak well of one another.
* Always defend one another.
* Allow no third person or influence into your relationship.
* Make sure you kiss one another every day, and touch one another every day.
* Find new ways to show that you love each other.
* Maintain your own identities so that you don't lose yourselves in the marriage, but always remain as one partnership.
* Seek out great challenges and adventures together.
* Your pasts bond you, but your future triumphs seal the bond.
* Respect each compartment of each other's lives...support the career, nurture the talents, feed the friendship, care for the home and the kids. Remember that you're both multi-faceted with many roles to fill.
* Never take each other for granted...not even the little things.

* When temptation calls, and it will, ask yourself if you're a man or woman of integrity...and then turn toward one another.
* The only thing in life that you can count on is change...so allow for changes to come and face them together.
* Keep the romance going...date one another even though you're married.
* Make time for one another in your schedules.
* Make each other your top priority.
* Share your dreams with one another; that's the only way you both can make them come true for each other.
* Live by the Golden Rule. It's so simple that we often forget it: do unto others as you would have them do unto you.
* Never get complacent.
* You need to earn one another's respect and love over and over.
* Look into each other's eyes right now and always remember what you see...then spend the rest of your life trying to make each other look like that.
* Ask one another for help, and allow the other to help you.
* Give plenty of compliments...you have no chance without them.
* Compliment one another to other people. Word always gets back.
* Care for yourselves personally so that you can be good partners to each other.

* When children come, remember that it's your strong marriage that nurtures them best.
* When you come home at night, always kiss your wife before you kiss the kids.
* Pray together and for each other.
* Surprise one another…even with the smallest thing or sentiment.
* Celebrate your milestones, your triumphs and achievements…toast one another's greatest moments.
* Fill your home with friends and family…it's the circle of loved ones around you that can make your partnership even better.
* The essence of a good marriage is compromise.
* Whatever you did to win one another over…keep doing it.
* Keep company with only good people.
* Never let a full day go by without hearing one another's voices.
* Just call to say hello.
* Love one another fully, in every aspect of the word.
* Follow your bliss.

Quotes to Inspire

"Nothing great was ever achieved without enthusiasm."
—Ralph Waldo Emerson

"Love has nothing to do with what you are expecting to get. Only with what you are expecting to give, which is everything."
—Katharine Hepburn

"Work like you don't need the money, love like you've never been hurt, dance like no one is watching."

—Kathy Mattea

"Joy has no cost."

—Marianne Williamson

"Marriage is not a ritual or an end. It is a long, intricate, intimate dance together, and nothing matters more than your own sense of balance and your choice of partner."

—Amy Bloom

"To improve is to change; to be perfect is to change often."

—Winston Churchill

A Note from the Author

You're on your way to creating a memorable speech that will bring tears of joy—and perhaps great laughter—to everyone's eyes. The bride and groom have entrusted you with the spotlight and with a golden moment on their wedding day, as they're sure your speech will fulfill all of their wishes and expectations...and then some. You've been chosen for your wit, your candor, your way with words, and also for the place you hold in their hearts. This is your moment to shine on their behalf and also add just a bit more sentiment to their day.

Whatever you say, they'll remember it forever.

Thank you for allowing me to help you on this important task. I know the incredible value of words and the expression of love and appreciation, as well as the place they can live forever in memories. I invite you to send in your masterfully written wedding toasts for future, updated editions of this book as well as my upcoming bridal articles. Please visit me at www.sharonnaylor.net to find out how you can be a part of my upcoming wedding projects.

I wish you a wonderful performance on the wedding day, the right words to say, and all the best in your own happy life of the future.

—Sharon Naylor

Your Wedding Toast Worksheet
1st Draft

_____

_____

_____

_____

_____

_____

_____

_____

_____

_____

_____

_____

Your Wedding Toast Worksheet
Final Version

(Note: Tear this page out and take it with you to the wedding.)

———————————————————

———————————————————

———————————————————

———————————————————

———————————————————

———————————————————

———————————————————

———————————————————

———————————————————

———————————————————

———————————————————

Wedding Toast Checklist

We are planning to include toasts...
___ to one another
___ to the bride
___ to the groom
___ to the bride's parents
___ to the groom's parents
___ to grandparents
___ to godparents
___ to the person/people who introduced us
___ to siblings
___ to best friends
___ to all of the guests present
___ to departed loved ones
___ to children of the marriage
___ to others:
___ to others:
___ to others:

We are planning to include toasts...
___ from the best man
___ from the groomsmen
___ from the maid/matron of honor
___ from the bridesmaids
___ from the bride's parents
___ from the groom's parents
___ from both sets of parents

___ from grandparents

___ from godparents

___ from guardians or other parental figures

___ from siblings

___ from friends

___ from children of the marriage

___ from others:

___ from others:

___ from others:

NOTES

About the Author

Sharon Naylor is the author of eighteen wedding books, including *Your Special Wedding Vows, The Complete Outdoor Wedding Planner, The Mother of the Bride Book, How to Have a Fabulous Wedding for $10,000 or Less, How to Plan an Elegant Wedding in Six Months or Less, The New Honeymoon Planner, The Ultimate Bridal Shower Idea Book*, and many others. She is also the co-author, along with celebrity bridal gown designers Michelle Roth and Henry Roth, of *Your Day, Your Way: The Essential Handbook for the 21st Century Bride.* She has written for *Bride's, Bridal Guide, Bride Again, Self, Shape, Health,* and many other magazines, and she is the online wedding questions consultant at www.njwedding.com. She lives in Madison, New Jersey, and is working on additional titles for the Sourcebooks wedding series.

If you would like to share your wedding stories for future editions of Sharon Naylor's books, or to learn more about the author, visit www.sharonnaylor.net.